❧ *Dora P. Chaplin* ❧

CHILDREN AND RELIGION

REVISED EDITION

WITH A FOREWORD

by Charles L. Taylor, Jr.

❧ *New York* ❧

CHARLES SCRIBNER'S SONS

T O

Adelaide Teague Case

9

Foreword

The late Archbishop Temple, when Headmaster of Repton, received a mother's request that her son substitute French for religious studies on the ground that it would be "better for him hereafter." Not all parents are equally certain of this; the more thoughtful wonder whether French or many another subject of the modern curriculum will fit their children for life in this turbulent time. In Professor Hocking's phrase, education in America is tragically deficient because it fails to expose souls, however generously endowed by nature, to what is "noble, generous, and faith-provoking." If God is the Creator, Sustainer, and Judge of the universe, if all things are "of Him and through Him and unto Him," then an education in which He is peripheral is eccentric education, and the sooner God occupies His rightful place in that education, the better for all his children "hereafter."

But how? Is the Sunday-School an answer? Can the Bible come alive in a child whose attention is already directed to comic strips, radio programs, sports news, and movie heroes? What books shall the child read, what books can help the parent to train the child to faith, hope, and charity? How shall the parent deal with disbelief? What is the method of leading a child into prayer? How help the child in the presence of death?

These are a few of the many questions to which Mrs. Chaplin replies. She answers them not only as a Director of Religious Education who has had extraordinary success, not only as a teacher who understands the psychology of childhood and youth, but as a parent who herself has been faced with the problems and driven by her own responsibility and care to find the best solutions available. In her quest she has had the help of Dr. Adelaide

vii

Foreword

Teague Case, who has read and commends her work, but whom illness has prevented from writing this foreword.

Mrs. Chaplin would be the last to pretend that her prescription tells the parent searching for a patent medicine how to rear a godly child. But another can say for her that perplexed men and women, looking for help as they seek to train their children in the knowledge and love of God and man, will find wisdom, frankness, humor, perspective, reality, kindly understanding and persuasive suggestion in this book.

CHARLES L. TAYLOR, JR.

Introduction to the Second Edition

The re-reading of a book written several years ago is a strange experience. In some ways it is like the perusal of work done by another person. Two things are likely to have happened in the years between two editions of a book: the face of the outer world may have changed, and the author (we hope) will have learned a little more about the topic.

In the case of CHILDREN AND RELIGION, I am surprised to find that the outer world it describes remains very much the same—only "more so." The hurry is there, mass media is influencing whole nations even more effectively and often demonically; the clouds of fear are still on the horizon. Certainly the urgency for more Christian work is more strongly felt. We have entered the atomic age. As I write, my eyes alight on the titles of two recent books on my desk: C. S. Lewis's *The World's Last Night,* and Romano Guardini's *The End of the Modern World.*

"Experts" in the field of education both religious and secular continue to argue about conflicting philosophies and methods. A whole new educational vocabulary has risen up, and now like all the others, it shows signs of being dethroned. But Christianity is Christ, and Christ does not change. In the midst of all the changing circumstances of a new civilization, the Church on earth as the gospel-bearing People of God, remains at worship and at work. The task is not different, the good news of man's creation by God and redemption in Christ is still ultimate truth. Christian parents and teachers continue to search for the best ways of interpreting that truth to the new generation.

Therefore, most of what I wrote before can stand, although like every author I wish it had been said better. It has all the limitations of having been said for Christians of many denomina-

Introduction to the Second Edition

tions, and my only reason for sending this volume on its way with a considerable number of revisions and a whole new bibliography, is that those teaching religion in the Church and in the home have been generous in their reception of it and have been kind enough to say it has helped them. It is, as you know, not a formally technical work and it is certainly not for scholars, although what is said I hope need not be unlearned, however far the reader travels afterwards. Its chief purpose is to give first thoughts, and to encourage the readers to study more deeply in other places. Nearly every story in it is true, and most of them grew out of encounters with my own children, so at least it has the virtue of not being "purely theoretical." When I wrote it I was less experienced than I am now, and for fear of not saying it strongly enough, I often quoted from the works of others. When one friend of mine was accused of doing this, he said to his assailants, "At least I read widely. Some people never quote because they never read!" In spite of his rejoinder, if I were to re-write the whole volume, I would probably say the same things in my own words.

"What would you do differently," I am sometimes asked, "if you were able to bring up your children all over again?" Many things. But above all I would be less reluctant to proclaim firmly what God has done so mightily "for us men and for our salvation." We were all influenced by the fear of "thrusting religion down our children's throats." While I am not advocating anything as violent as that, I beg parents to remember that we are not born with a foreknowledge of what God has done. He has already acted. And someone must tell us. So be strong and of good courage. There are hard times ahead, but Christ has overcome the world.

DORA P. CHAPLIN

The General Theological Seminary, New York.
August 1960

Introduction to the First Edition

It's hard to believe in God if your parents don't," wrote a Seventh Grade boy recently, in a short sermon his class was preparing to give in Church.

We pride ourselves on being conscientious parents, but if the religious education of our children is left to chance, are we being fair to them?

There is so much talk of the hopeless materialism of our age that there is a danger that we may stop our ears to shut out the weary repetition. This does not alter facts. The new generation is here, and we are bound to help it rediscover what was lost. We have worshipped success, humanism, politics, money, self-expression. Each in turn has proved useless in a world where the thoughtful are haunted by images of ruined cities, scarred fields, and starving children. Our minds, like men and nations, are confused and divided. Many of us are haunted by the knowledge that within the next few years world society must lay hold of a moral way of life—or perish. This is written in the conviction that the moral life is rooted in religion. We must rediscover the life of the spirit or die.

If we agree on this the next thing is to do something about it. This book is an attempt to outline the potential religious growth of children in a troubled world, and to offer practical suggestions to parents and teachers who can help them to realize the only heritage of which no man can rob them—a growing faith in God. I write in humility, aware of the magnitude of the task.

Gratitude and appreciation go to my teacher, Dr. Adelaide Case, without whose encouragement we would not have set out to try to make some of these ideas a reality in a Parish School; to Rev. Cornelius P. Trowbridge, who had confidence in our beginnings in Chestnut Hill; and to the Rev. John T. Golding, whose faith and inspiration is a cause for the hope that the teaching power of the Church may go forward.

I have no thanks adequate for the loyalty of the teachers and parents with whom I have worked, busy people who have given time to help lay the foundations of the Church School we hope for; also for those unable to leave young families, who know that the heart of religion is in the home. Among these people, Mr. Henry Keyes has been my right arm throughout the venture, revealing a genius for teaching energic boys, and an insight into the many problems that continue to assail us. I am indebted to him for quotations from his lessons and reports; to another teacher, Mr. Dows Dunham, Egyptologist at the Museum of Fine Arts, Boston, for his lesson on page 102; and to Mrs. Clarence Severy, whose devoted work brought new life to a discouraged class. Last, but certainly not least, I must acknowledge the unfailing help of our Vestry, who, recognizing the urgency and importance of Christian Education, have made it their greatest concern in the affairs of one Parish.

There is much to be done, the time is short; but we can work.

DORA P. CHAPLIN

Chestnut Hill, Massachusetts.
January 1948

Contents

CHILDREN AND RELIGION

CHAPTER ONE

The Need of Our Time

"If you want a description of our age, here is one. The civilization of means without ends; rich in means beyond any other epoch, and almost beyond human needs; squandering and misusing them, because it has no overruling ideal: an ample body with a meager soul. . . . Science and politics are essential but they are not enough without the spiritual strand, which, using the word in its widest sense, we may call religion."

—SIR RICHARD LIVINGSTONE
[from *On Education*, Macmillan]
Copyright 1944. By permission

We have been called the prisoners of our age. When our children are born into the world we resolve to give them the best we know, and then we find that we are all caught in the mesh of time; we stand where all humanity stands. Without some sword of the spirit we cannot move away from where we find ourselves.

Those of us who grew up in the years following the first World War know that it was not fashionable to be enthusiastic about anything. If we dared to be, our contemporaries turned upon us with contempt and said we were

I

"intense." So we pretended to scorn this or that: ours was to be an age of realism; we would not have dust cast into our eyes as our forefathers had done. This period was vulgarly known as the "debunking" era. Science and psychology were our strong and willing allies. We could not see at that time that although psychiatry disentangled some of our thinking, it could not give us a better pattern for the remaking of our lives.

In a previous century Goethe had said:

> To understand the living whole,
> They start by driving out the soul;
> They count the parts, and when all's done,
> Alas! the spirit-bond is gone.

Such a tremendous force of scientific opinion had carried us along that mystery had been almost driven out of our lives. "Surely these forces must be the lords of the universe," we said to ourselves.

It would be foolish to depreciate our debts to science, when life itself is so greatly enriched by its discoveries and through it comes our longer expectation of life; nor must we fail to appreciate what wise psychology has done towards clearing the ground for a deeper understanding of the human mind; but for a time we were tricked into thinking that scientific laws were the All of existence. "There is nothing that can free us from this bond," says Jung, "except that opposite urge of life, the spirit. It is not the children of the flesh, but the 'children of God' who know freedom. In Ernst Barlach's tragic novel of family life, *Der Tote Tag*, the mother-daemon says at the end: 'The strange thing is that man will not learn that God is his father.' . . . We moderns are faced with the necessity of rediscovering the

life of the spirit; we must experience it anew for ourselves." [1] He goes on to admit a living Spirit in our lives.
"This is wonderful," I thought. "We are going to be allowed
to believe in God after all."

The president of a great convention attended by young
psychiatrists from all over the country approached them
tentatively with the conviction at which he had arrived,
namely, that their work should now take a religious turn.
To his intense relief, he found they had already arrived at
the same conclusion and were not ashamed to admit it.

Many scientists, too, have moved towards this conclusion,
and stand bewildered before laws which are a greater mystery than the wonders proceeding from them. If only man
will seek humbly, will it not be possible as the generations
move forward to tap the sources of spiritual power which
lie around us, and are ready if we find the key? Life holds
inestimably more than the intellect can evolve from it; we
need to find a more noble way of interpreting its values,
"For where your treasure is, there shall your heart be also."
The seed of spiritual experience which lies at the core of
life does not grow of itself, but given sunshine and rain the
mystery within it will stir.

From thinkers all over the world come words which sound
like prophecies. They vary considerably in their optimism.
Take, for instances, these three statements made in deep
sincerity by an educator, a churchman, and the press:

Sir Richard Livingstone writing on education, says: "During the last war the salvation of the world was assigned to
Science. Now we are disillusioned. Science, like medicine,
is an integral part of civilized life. It is difficult to maintain
health without doctors, but medicine is not health. It is

[1] Jung, C. G., *Modern Man in Search of a Soul*, p. 140.

difficult for a civilization to be sound without science, but science is not civilization, and few people can suppose that salvation is its business. Today we tend to assign that rôle to psychology, economics and sociology. These branches of knowledge are indispensable to our civilization. We have not enough of them. We need more. But the adjuncts and auxiliaries, they too are not the Saviors of society, and if we fix our hopes on them future years will find us further down the hill and looking for some other force to help us recover our lost ground. . . . The forces that move the world need to be informed and disciplined by the intellect, but they are not in themselves intellectual." [2]

That same year Archbishop Temple said, "The world is learning its helplessness apart from God, though not yet is it on any great scale turning to Him for direction or for strength." And a year later: "The Christian tradition is challenged from without more powerfully than in any period since the end of the Dark Ages, and is in danger of being undermined by a secular humanism which hopes to retain Christian values without Christian faith." [3]

On August 8, 1945, just after the announcement of the use of the atomic bomb, came these words in the leader of a daily newspaper: "This is a human invention. As with gunpowder, the armored ship, the airplane and the submarine, it will become a weapon available to aggressors and non-aggressors alike. Only the sword of Michael—spiritual strength—fights for the good alone. . . . Until men understand that the 'weapons of our warfare are not carnal' they will struggle along to defend themselves with such counter-

[2] *On Education,* Essay I, p. 118; Essay II, p. 63, Macmillan.
[3] *The Church Looks Forward,* pp. 1, 9, Macmillan. Copyright 1944. By permission.

4

feits of the Divine Power. But the atomic bomb should— not only by the awfulness of its self-destructive force but by the horrible inhumanity its use involves—jar us into a keener awareness for the necessity for winning peace through understanding the one spiritual Power." [4]

Those of us who are faced with the privilege and responsibility of bringing up children are sometimes tempted to look backward and wish for a slower pace and what seemed to us the surer ways of our own childhood, or possibly that of our mothers. We read, perhaps, a family letter of long ago, written in the days when correspondence was a pleasant art now so largely superseded by the telephone or made unnecessary by rapid travel, and we think how much easier it must have been to live in those more leisurely times. Although in some respects we were not so comfortable in material ways, great nations did not fall overnight, and the events of history did not carry us along in a whirlwind. No sooner have we recovered our breath, but some other stupendous event leaves us gasping and wondering what is coming next; maps of the world change, the boundaries of nations are moved. We remark rather feebly that the world is getting smaller as we find out that journeys which took weeks twenty years ago are now being accomplished in days, or even hours.

Surely these stones which have been flung into the quieter waters of our childhood will go on making ripples for decades to come, and these disturbances are deep; change has come and will go on, it is for us to decide whether it will be productive of good or of evil.

In other countries there are millions of young people who have had no childhood, who have been reared in fear, hatred,

[4] *Christian Science Monitor*, Aug. 8, 1945, Atlantic Edition.

and starvation. The best thought in America is disturbed at the trend of education today.

Where are we going? What do we want? What is wrong with the old, and why do we look for the new? This is not a worn-out world, we are told, see what vigor is shown in industry and science. Even at the risk of being obvious, it is necessary to see where we stand. The most thoughtful people of our time refuse to live in a fool's paradise about the future; but in other places there is a desperate danger that, with the military victory of the Second World War, we shall rest on our oars and find ourselves once again overcome.

Throughout the ages men have needed a vision, and having seen it, have been ready to follow it. Sometimes they saw it "through a glass darkly," as in Germany, but they follow it just the same. What we need in America and England today is a clear vision, for without it "the people perish." From time to time we think we have found one—science, sociology, new orders—but because we do not weld them together with spiritual strength they alone cannot save our civilization from disaster.

We are being told that we are living on the spiritual capital of our ancestors, and capital unreplenished does not last forever. Even if we take a more optimistic view, and concede that the forms of Christianity change and are reinterpreted in each successive generation, we are not encouraged by what we see. The rise in juvenile delinquency, those in authority tell us, is not due to wars only; there is in many cases a lack of interest and responsibility on the part of the parents, a lack not confined to any one income level. We also know by the terrible numbers of patients in our mental and neurological centers that something is wrong.

The Need of Our Time

A great doctor once said he never had to psychoanalyze a patient with a satisfying religious life, adding that a purely humanistic religion could not be classified as satisfactory.

There are, of course, in every age some shining souls who are the exception, but those dealing with college students will testify that these young people, on the whole, have no ruling philosophy of life, clear values, or definite standards. We ask ourselves as parents and teachers, how are these values to be learned? They are being meted out to our children constantly by television, radio, the movies, advertisements, and the public press; in fact they descend upon the modern child almost from the cradle, in all he sees and in all he hears. I am not condemning these things, I believe most of them have come to stay and we had better learn how to use them constructively, but by the time college age is reached the majority of students who, according to conventional standards, are "well-educated" have no fixed stars to steer by. The inner conflict may be hidden, but it has been repeatedly proved that failure in these years is more often due to this inner tension than it is attributable to lack of mental powers or to indolence.

And what of the millions of young people who do not go to college, and of those who do not even graduate from High School? Why are so many adolescents listless and disillusioned? In their childhood these people showed eager joy and curiosity.

The spiritual capital of which we spoke will not remain with us forever: most of us enjoy the Christian legacy without stopping to think where it came from. Recently I heard a fine preacher say at a conference, speaking to the students in their own language, "Christianity won't just stay around like Stonehenge, you know!" We had better realize before it is too late that Christianity and materialism are locked in a desperate struggle: it is not enough for us to stand and cheer on the fight, we had better enter the lists—parents, teachers, Everyman.

It is said that when Viscount Bryce was asked what he considered would be the effect of having religious education removed from the school curriculum, he replied, "I can't answer that until three generations have passed." Now the generations are passing, and a professor at one of our outstanding universities told me the other day that if he makes such a remark as "a camel going through the eye of a needle" the class laughs heartily at his original wit. We may shrug our shoulders at the idea of losing the principles of Christianity in our midst, and we may say only the pessimists talk that way—but what of Germany? What good German of our grandparents' day would have countenanced the prophecy that the time would come when mass-killings, torture, and concentration camps would darken their land? If the spirit of Christianity had been as well-organized as that of Hitlerism, and as captivating to the soul of youth, these horrors could not have been.

The majority of parents are anxious to do their best for their children. Our country spends vast sums on education; we have some of the finest school buildings in the world. Are they being used in the best way?

Men who through active fighting have become acquainted with the misery of war are often the prophets we need. "The man who has lived with death from day to day," wrote one of them from the battlefield, "is initiated by suffering into the power of simple truths; he knows what human helplessness can really be like, and he knows too what the power of the spirit can do."

From the pen of a chaplain in the Pacific came these accusing words: "American education lacks any realistic approach to international life and politics, as well as ordinary courses in philosophy and religion, let alone orientation in the specifically Christian attitude toward self and society. In fact, there is little in American education, whether religious or secular, that can give men a sustained dynamic for a tragic world." [5]

We strive hard to give vocational education to our children; we want them to be happy and successful socially; but if, in spite of many virtues, they have no working faith to apply to the problems of life, we have failed them, for they can never grow to their full stature without a vision of God. If they can gain that insight, then they are indeed fortunate to be alive in a time when a great new civilization could be built.

If we want world peace we must work towards some spiritual bond between the nations, only from this unity can come the final renunciation of war. Our country today has been likened to a good machine with no power to set it in motion.

On the credit side of this serious debt to our children, we may realize that in many ways we are better equipped than the generations of the past: much delving and clearing has been done by wise psychology; there is a growing restlessness and enquiry, humanity wants to be guided towards what have been called "the enduring sources of regeneration." We are beginning to understand how the *natural* processes of the human mind are related to religion.

Noted psychologists have come to believe that religion is the only effective basis for building an integrated person-

[5] Clarence Kilde, in *Christianity and Crisis*, Jan. 8, 1945.

ality; so assuredly is it the most urgent need of the world today, to utilize all the growing power in the mind and heart of mankind, to find a moral and spiritual reality in so doing, and in working toward the integrated life of the individual, to travel toward an integrated world.

Because it seems abundantly clear that the heart of religion is in the home, and that parents and teachers are those on whom the responsibility of things to come lies heaviest; because education is an atmosphere and a life begun and continued at home and at school; and finally because the most potent influence in a child's religious life is his parents' attitude towards good and evil, for without faith and example we can accomplish nothing—this book is a humble attempt to discover how we can give life more abundantly to the new generation, while rediscovering life ourselves. In the hands of those satisfied with things as they are, it will find no place.

When the United Nations Charter was ratified, these words came in the opening prayer, when reference was made to "this strange world where no good thing comes save as we fulfil the conditions of its coming." We shall try to discover the best conditions for the education of the spirit: on this rests the fate of our civilization.

CHAPTER TWO

Three Stages of Growth

Only the feet that move in order dance;
Only the mind attuned to that dread pulse
Of law, throughout the universe, can sing.
Only the soul that plays its rhythmic part
In that great measure of the tides and suns
Terrestrial and celestial, till it soar
Into the supreme melodies of heaven,
Only that soul, climbing the splendid road
Of law, from height to height, may walk with God,
Shape its own sphere from chaos, conquer death,
Lay hold on life and liberty, and sing.
—ALFRED NOYES

Half-knowledge is said to be worse than ignorance. One sometimes wonders whether psychology books should be forbidden to parents, perhaps even to young teachers. This is a terrible heresy but—when we have watched the effects on earnest parents of dabbling in these books, or seen the strained and reverent attention bestowed upon them by certain student teachers who are being taught to label Johnnie and Mary, putting both them and their actions and reactions into neat little pigeonholes where they refuse to stay—we wonder again.

Children and Religion

A friend of mine who was staying with a group of writers and artists some years ago, when all the world was reading Freud, told me how he was once eating breakfast at the same table as the poet, Edwin Arlington Robinson. There were several of them, and they were eventually joined by an effusive lady, known to be both sentimental and gloriously ignorant. She broke into the general conversation telling them how sure she was that they would like to hear about the wonderful dreams she had had the previous night, and she plunged into a long description of them. When she stopped there was a tense silence. After some awkward moments, the poet put out his hand and rang the little table bell. The waitress came, and said:

"What can I do for you, Mr. Robinson?"

"Oh, nothing thank you," said the poet. "I just felt I wanted to ring a bell."

We too have often felt we would like to ring a bell and silence some of the chatter about children and their ways. On the other hand, if we look more deeply into the question, and realize that many parents approach the idea of amateur psychology with gaiety and good sense, we may avoid some of the pitfalls which a superficial knowledge of any subject is liable to present.

Psychology is a comparatively young science. In the past twenty years it has undergone radical changes. We must remember the vast output of textbooks on the subject. In 1930 a man going into a public library asked to see a book on psychology written in 1929. He was led to a shelf which extended from one end of the room to the other—all these, the librarian said, had been written that year.

Those who taught at the peak of each particular phase

were impregnated with those particular ideas, and some of them remain so, teaching what they believe to be true, but what is in reality twenty years behind the heights reached by outstanding men in the field. You will find in turn the Freudians, the Behaviorists, the devotees of Adler, and the followers of Jung.

It is interesting to see how their teachings invade our homes. As a very humble illustration, I recall that when my first baby was born I was instructed with severity to "let her cry, and don't play with her except at mothering time," because of the grave effect it might have on her infant ego. Two years later, in time for the next baby, there was a new axiom: "Security. Security is what the child needs above all things. Give your baby all the mothering it wants."

Almost every new discovery has a grain of truth in it, and we have to use common sense to keep the balance. We have seen that we must not despise the delving and sifting done by wise psychologists, and we must acknowledge the fact that many a difficulty has been straightened out by applying the results of their research. The fact that we are still groping in dim light for the laws governing the human mind does not mean that they are non-existent, only that we are slow in discovering them, and frequently interpret them wrongly.

What does concern us tremendously is the fact that, although some exponents continue to disagree, the greatest of them, as they penetrate more deeply into the mysteries of human personality, are becoming urgently aware of the need for a religiously inclined life in every individual. They find it necessary, not only for the "soul's health," but for that maturity and integration of personality, without which we cannot reach the heights of usefulness or happiness of which we are capable, and we have no true realization of life.

Dr. Jung found, when going over his records, that nearly all his patients were suffering from a loss of religious faith, and that when this was restored they regained their mental health. All this is stated in his *Modern Man in Search of a Soul*. And Professor Yeaxlee tells how Jung, when asked at an international conference whether he considered the religious experience valid, answered most emphatically, "Yes," and said that without it we are a little insane.

It is not the purpose of this book to attempt to trace the psychologist's struggle to reach this vital conclusion, but those parents and teachers who are interested will find it surveyed most fairly in Basil Yeaxlee's *Religion and the Growing Mind*.[1] Faith is likely to be reinforced rather than shaken, for this book is scrupulously fair, and shows the contribution of many who have worked faithfully to discover the truth.

Every child's life develops a dominating purpose. That purpose we may call his religion, for he will be religious to the extent that it dominates him. Our problem has been summed up for us, "It is not a question as to whether a man shall be religious, but what religion shall dominate him?"

Because we want to see that religion as part of his natural growth, it will help us to look at his development in three broad stages, for everything we consider in this book will be associated with them, because we are trying, not to enforce something from outside, but to nourish what is al-

[1] Seabury Press.

ready there. We will try to find out what plays the greatest part in the formation of character and the shaping of purpose, we will try to show him both good and evil, and to foster a strenuous desire to choose the good.

It is not sensible to make exact age barriers because of the great difference in the rate of development, but the ones we are used to considering, for the sake of clarity, are approximately: the young child, that is, the infant to about seven years old; the older children, of seven to eleven years; and the adolescents, who in themselves are now allowed three steps, generally called

Early adolescence .... 12–15 years
Middle adolescence .... 15–18 years
Late adolescence .... Early Twenties

We all know the young child with his great capacity for wonder, a readiness to learn, and an almost inexhaustible energy. He has a perpetual curiosity. He is very busy getting acquainted with himself. In our next chapter, on the home, we shall see again how very early the religious education of a child is all-unconsciously begun. Here we want to survey him, as it were, at a distance.

We find that he lives half in and half out of fairyland, much of his time in a world of fantasy, which will vary according to his background. He can pretend to be any character in his play he wants. He enjoys hearing stories and he loves to tell them.

We cannot be too much on our guard in assuring ourselves that the story has gone over, in its important points, as we intended. That is why it is good to have our stories "told back" to us. In Chapter Nine we refer to the mistaken nomenclature of hymns. An adult may think he has told a fine tale to the young and receive certain shocks when it is repeated.

A five-year-old told me joyfully that she had heard the most wonderful story about a gorgeous pirate, who upon investigation proved to be none other than Pontius Pilate himself. The seven-year-old daughter of a minister informed her assembled family at Sunday dinner that she had heard "a most lovely story at Sunday school about a man called Solomon who had a wife and quite forty porcupines."

After this we meet, somewhere along the road between seven and eleven, the Juniors. They have tremendous physical and mental energy; their curiosity, which we must turn to account for wide uses, continues to be great. These children like to have responsibilities in family life and in the church, and they wonder about world problems. They become more matter-of-fact, but they are suggestible, and if we do not destroy their powers, they will keep the shining gifts of their earlier childhood. They become increasingly social and will soon become devoted to their friends in "clubs" and "gangs."

The Junior is growing interested in the *outer* world, he is discovering a new world for himself, different from his fantasy one, but if he is given a chance he finds it as wonderful. "Is it true?" he will ask, when you tell him a story. He does not mind if you say "No," but he wants to keep fact and fantasy divided in his mind. By all means let him have legend and myth, but give him history too.

From his religious teaching the Juniors enjoy discovering how Abraham went out from Ur of the Chaldees to look for the Unknown God, and they discover, too, the special revelation of our monotheistic religion. They begin to see the wonder of these great patriarchs and prophets in the light of the Unknown God they are searching for. I think that they should know quite early that we are not absolutely certain that the man who first set out from Ur was called Abraham—what matters is that some brave leader set out to guide the people. He had the courage and the conviction to go forward, and it was what this man stood for that was more important than the name we happened to use.

In the same way, the wonderful stories of the Creation can be told, as George Hodges does in his *Garden of Eden,* as the ones probably listened to by families around their campfires in the old nomadic days when they made their long journey to Canaan, and perhaps a child asked, "How was the world made?"

These children have most probably had tales of the gods and heroes at day school, and they like to carry on from where the legends end. They have a keen interest in other countries, and when we explore the Old Testament we find Joseph enslaved in the Egypt they are wandering in in their geography lessons. This ability to correlate their knowledge is a priceless thing in the building of a religious faith.

The Junior wants to see, as he nears adolescence, some of the practical workings of the Christian religion, and he wants to have strong heroes. Sometimes he wants to know what modern men have done to aid the search—missionaries and great men like Pastor Niemöller who have stood up courageously in conquered lands. As time goes on, the daily papers give news of Christians in our own country and abroad, who are 'spokesmen for God' in a clash of world forces. The Junior is looking for a *certainty of God.*

The children of this age begin to love to argue: they will

go on indefinitely in pure enjoyment of the battle. As the years go by they frequently appear to be cock-sure and overbearing. We must be patient. They are not at all sure of this world they are finding, and this attitude is a defense. They are looking for reality.

Despite all this, if the young child has been given a wise beginning, he can come to later childhood with a very real sense of the presence of God, and be completely unselfconscious about it in the presence of those he believes will understand. To others, I suppose he says nothing.

A lively eight-year-old once sat next to me in church when the minister was saying in a reassuring voice, "God is very near us. He is only in the next room."

She whispered to me in a surprised and slightly anxious voice, "Why does he say that? God is right here beside us."

In the past, the adolescent and the little child have received much more attention than the Junior. There is a growing conviction that the study of this important age has been neglected, and its bearing upon future development underestimated. I believe that if a sane intellectual and historic basis can be given for some of our religious beliefs *before* the tensions of adolescence set in, and if the child can see, however dimly, where his service is needed in the pattern of history, there is much less likely to be a breakdown of faith and a rejection of religion as a beautiful fairy tale belonging to old people and invalids, not to lively girls and virile boys.

And now for the much-discussed adolescent himself. He refuses to keep to the book and grow tidily in the lines and boundaries set forth for him. Presently we shall give him a whole chapter to himself, and his relation to the home;

here we want to see how he fits into the first outline we are making of the steps in human growth.

When our age gets into double figures, especially as the teens are entered, it becomes increasingly difficult for us to look back honestly at our own experiences. Of this, Eleanor Acland says, "Self-consciousness, arch enemy of veracity, begins to distort the memory. Which of us could, even if we would, set down a frank record of our adolescence? For most of us its actual passage was such an incomprehensible medley that, looking back at it from a distance, the colors of the pictures that survive, have, so to speak, run and smudged. Moreover, our recollections are overlaid with an accretion of adult ideas about ourselves and life in general which makes it difficult to be sure what the original genuine coloring of the thoughts and feelings of the years of indiscretion may have been." [2]

It is not usually an easy time for the adults who live with him, less so for the adolescent himself. We feel that the teen-ager is one minute a child, and the next moment a grown-up. In spite of all our good resolutions, that is the way we treat him. We say, for example, "Why can't you put the key of the garage back where it belongs? A great boy of your age ought to be able to remember a simple thing like that!"

A few minutes later we hear ourselves remarking, "Stay out as late as that? I should think not. When you are older that will be another matter, but while you are only so-and-so you will have to do what I say."

This is the critical time when the inner conflict is so often hidden. This is the time when, as we said in our first

[2] *Goodbye for the Present,* p. 112, Hodder & Stoughton.

chapter, failure at school or college comes, not because of laziness or lack of ability, but because of the stress and strain of these most difficult years. He needs contact with adults who are a valiant example, whose arguments are systematic and whose thinking is clear.

Just before early adolescence the Junior puts on a great spurt of growth. His body changes rapidly. As early adolescence is reached he often feels clumsy and self-conscious, he tries to adapt himself to his sudden growth, and we are told that the fact that there is a slight difference between the rate of muscular growth and nervous control adds to his difficulties of co-ordination. This aspect has been overdone in journalism and on the screen. We forget that at this time the sensibilities are also quickened, and the sense of beauty is keener. They know "the heights of idealism, and the depths of despair."

One of them writes:

> I have no words;
> I can only watch the thin buds on the trees
> Bursting into speech, making the seasons.
> I have no song:
> I am only a listener to the notes of Time in my blood,
> But I can make no music out of it.
> When myself, tall as the world, has ceased to confront me,
> I will perhaps tell of what I have seen,
> I too will share in the making of seasons.[3]

It has been said that life is difficult for most people, and tragic for many by the time they are thirty. If we accept this, and instead of telling young people about the brave new world that is coming, try to fit them to meet whatever disas-

[3] Jean Shepard, in *John o' London's Weekly*.

ter lies ahead, while we help them to forge a sword of the spirit with which they may fight for the Kingdom of God, we shall be better able to help our children to acquire a working faith applicable to life's problems.

The adolescent must adjust to the new world he is discovering, as the Junior did to his. There is a feeling of personal frustration which comes as he slowly perceives the predicament of modern man. He is rightly impatient with things as they are.

Dr. Adelaide Case, in an article on "Religion and Maturity," said, "Only as personality matures in adolescence can the active concern for human need which is so central in religion take on real significance, for only then can the tragic circumstances of others be to any real sense understood and assimilated." [4]

However, we are not at this point trying to do more than draw the outline of general growth in very wide sweeps, so that when we examine religious development we can decide whether it is in harmony with natural development and deep need.

School work is often piled on at this time; though actually the years of early adolescence are not the best for academic learning, the child is too distracted by his new self. He will not discover this new self unless we give him opportunities for service. This is the moment when he must "lose himself that he may find himself." He is sensitive to jobs invented for him for the good of his soul. We must find real needs in the community in which we live.

The headmaster of a boarding school in Scotland tells how he tried to interest his boys in building a hut as a lookout on a coast dangerous to fishermen. He says he met

---

[4] *Current Religious Thought,* June 1945.

with passive resistance, the boys were suspicious. Just then a government official came down to thank them for their interest and offered to put in a telephone to help control the unwatched area, if they would build the hut. Finding the need genuine, he says they set to work in the worst part of the winter, and had it finished in a short time.

In middle adolescence young people try to consolidate what they know, and the mental powers are said to be at their height. In a few years they will go out into the adult world, how soon depending on the plans for their life and the circumstances around them. They are looking, perhaps quite unconsciously, for a pattern that makes sense, some light by which they can live and work in the long years ahead. They want adventure too. And even more than the younger ones, they want to create something to better conditions as they find them.

Of us they will become acutely critical, and all our thoughts and ways will come under the searchlight of their minds. Woe betide us, and the religious life we are hoping to inspire, if we prove ourselves afraid of new ideas or refuse to look at our beliefs in the light of modern criticism. The awful responsibility of guiding these growing years and of trying to have the right influences brought to bear upon them rests upon us. But there comes a stage, usually somewhere in the middle adolescence or earlier, when we simply have to sit back and watch the child making mistakes. We had our chance during those earlier years when we tried to build on a rock. Now we need to try to surround them with leaders who are going in the right direction, for John and Mary are going to pay more attention to outside influence than to us. Whether they can discern the true and the false among their elders and their contemporaries depends very largely on the standards which were built earlier. With the weight thus resting upon us, we wonder how we ever dared become parents!

Last comes maturity, somewhere in the twenties. The cynic will tell us this is sometimes never reached. This is the time when the personality begins to find unification in life and service to which all the powers may be dedicated. He finds "the remedy of a single heart," called by Jesus "purity of heart." If he has through worship and work come to know what it means to be a part of the creativity of God, no tempest can shake him.

CHAPTER THREE

The Home and the Younger Child

"We have not infected our youngsters with a sense of vocation, of dedication, of a purpose and aim above the passive ones of conspicuous consumption. We have made their goals that of the cabbage, a nutritive drawing-in . . . or at best, perhaps, that of the squirrel that collects and hoards, rather than the vision of the end of man which is to create and to build. If they are sub-humanoid it is because we are also. If their present aim in life is to have a more costly sweater than Mary Jones perhaps it is because our aim in life is to have a more costly automobile than Jonathan Jones."

—WILFORD O. CROSS
in *The Witness*, January 2, 1958

We must now face the charges made as to the effects of our own lives upon the religious growth of our children. We can try to discover just how this takes place, and how they are affected by our attitudes in a world that does not promise to be a very easy place to grow up in.

Reading certain books on religious education written as recently as twenty years ago, we wonder just how to apply their principles to our own children. The problem of our times seems to be how to find a golden way between exposing them ruthlessly to the less desirable influences of modern life and shielding them too much, so that they become perfect prigs, disliked and teased by their contemporaries. The child's moral code is absorbed, almost as the atmosphere is breathed: he does not choose it himself. It comes to him through home and friends, church and school, and through the influences we have already mentioned: the unworthy ones are often bad movies, advertisements, poor picture books and funny papers, and the public press. We cannot shield him from those. I have come to the conclusion that our job is to give him a standard, to help him from our side of the picture by offering him the finest books, pictures, and poetry. The good school will also do this. In the rough and tumble of school life with his contemporaries he will also get enough of imperfection to inoculate his system against the holier-than-thou attitude: his friends will take care of that. Religion has been defined as "the desire and ability to worship God, and to love and serve one's neighbor," but there is no beautiful equation whereby one can promise that given a particular set of prayers or books, we shall then be certain of developing a religious life within our children. Nor is it enough to send them to good day schools and excellent church schools while we sit back and hope for the best.

We come back continuously to the same inescapable fact. It is what we ARE, not what we SAY, which will effect the children most. In an atmosphere of continual criticism, how can the idea of the love of God be understood? Those working with children in some districts find that if the idea of God as a Father is suggested it immediately brings up thoughts of cruelty and injustice. The very word God has been heard by some only in swearing. This is not confined to any one section of the community. In a great variety of places you can find children today whose ideas of God are so hazy as to be almost non-existent.

In most schools, the name of Christ is not mentioned and religion is not discussed. I am speaking of the average day school—not those run by certain churches, or by the Society of Friends, for in those there is an attempt to give what is described as "a religiously-guarded education." Because of this children think of religion as an extra-curriculum activity, or they do not think of it at all.

Recently I heard a minister make a plea to his congregation on these lines:

"There is a story of a man who was brought in Court and when the title of the case was read out, 'The State versus John Smith,' he was heard to say: 'My God, what a majority.' Well, there is a terrific majority of secular influence ranged against the attempt that is being made to give a spiritual interpretation of life to our children. We know the reason why religious instruction has not been given in the public schools. We know that the responsibility rests upon the churches who couldn't agree upon what should be taught. . . . The result is that millions of American children are growing up without any religious instruction. We talk about the need for instructing the youth of other countries along Christian lines. We had better talk and think a bit more about the need of educating the youth of America along Christian lines. Two boys who were above the average in their day school came to a church school. One of them, when he was asked about Jesus, answered that he thought He was one of the saints. The other had never heard of Him. Unless the tide of secularism is stopped and unless something far more efficient is done to lay a Christian foundation for the future, our children and our grandchildren are going to grow up in a nation that is largely pagan." [1]

He went on to stress that neither church nor school could accomplish much without the co-operation of the home because the home lays the foundation of habits and attitudes and ideals upon which the church and the school must build. "Parents," he said, "lean over backwards to be fair. They say they don't want to force religion on anyone else. But I submit that it isn't fair to leave this decision to children before they are old enough to understand what is involved. I submit it isn't fair to let any child grow up without knowing who Christ was and what He taught and what His influence has been upon the world. I believe there is something in the quality of Christ which appeals to boys and girls just as truly today as it did to that boy beside the lake so many years ago in Galilee."

There was once a church school teacher who prayed, "Lord, help me to live so that even the youngest child will know what I mean when I teach." It is influence rather than instruction that we can offer in the very early years: later we try to offer both.

Loving kindness is something a baby can sense very early. We ourselves do not deny the subtle thing called atmosphere that we feel immediately we enter a house. We are not all equally sensitive to it, neither are tiny babies all equally sensitive to the moods and tones around them, but many are acutely so, and all seem to have some measure of perception. We have seen that the baby's unconscious idea of parental personality lead to his ideas of God.

[1] The Rev. Cornelius P. Trowbridge.

27

Children and Religion

Kneeling down each night beside a baby's bed and saying a prayer may not seem to us to have an important influence upon such a tiny child, but as the months go on, this calls forth, in some mysterious way, a feeling of love and reverence in the child, long before he is able to think. As times goes on and he is able to speak, he asks about the One to whom the prayers are said. This is the natural way to hear about God. Later in the book we describe the opposite method, when, with a clearing of the throat, the adult decides that it is high time we talked about God. The child may ask who it is you are talking to. Most mothers and fathers tell little children that they are talking to God, a loving Father who gave them all the people they love, and the lovely things we can see. This Heavenly Father likes to be spoken to, and loves the child even more than his parents do. Of course all this develops very slowly.

If you are not quite happy in your own mind about the early introduction of the word God, to which certain thoughtful people object, you can read a scholarly defense in Professor Yeaxlee's book already mentioned. My own very simple defense is that if the child does not hear the word "God" from you, and if you do not try to have the word grow in slow beauty for him, he will certainly hear it before long elsewhere, in unexpected and unfortunate ways.

The child having felt that God is like a father and a mother, but even more loving, we have seen that we have to try to live those qualities which we would have him associate with parenthood. But we must be honest. It is better not to be an artificial saint. We are not going to pretend to be perfect or to know everything. It does help

if we can say, "I don't know. Let's try to find out together."
Or, "I don't think anyone knows the answer to that. Perhaps some day you will be one of those people who helped find out."

As the child grows older he will ask questions that have baffled the theologians and philosophers of all time. He is likely to do this at dinner, or in the bath-tub, which probably because of its relaxing influence is conducive to profound thinking—and we must be ready.

"What does God look like?" is one of the most usual questions. "We don't know what he looks like, but we believe we know what He cares about," is an answer sometimes given. They often ask *how* we know what God cares about. For this there seems only one true answer, and this thought we need to keep before the child at all times. "Jesus came to show us what God is like," and "We know what God cares about because we know what Jesus cared about."

Some children do not ask questions for a long time; others will begin as soon as they can string sentences together, and by the time they are five years old they have expressed some very deep problems indeed. A five-year-old girl inquired, "I know God makes Himself, but how does He fetch the things to make Himself with?"

We must help as far as we can, and although we must never use this as an escape from hard thinking, it would seem to me that we sometimes have to say that while we live in this world we have a certain kind of mind, and perhaps there are some things which are just too big for us to understand until we move on.

I think we should answer honestly and exactly as far as

we are able. Children understand so much more than we give them credit for. Ernst Lothar, in his delicate little study of his two daughters, says:

"There are people who answer children's questions with, 'You can't understand that.' They always amazed me. Did they consider childhood the theater for a half-conscious existence of the picture-book size? Couldn't they see it is the stage for the very same comedies and tragedies as those of the adults, only happier and sadder, since the children's world is still experienced exclusively through feeling that minimizes nothing and enlarges everything human? Children understand everything." [2]

So, in quiet talks with their parents or a trusted teacher, little philosophers will ask one tremendous question after another if they are of that turn of mind. Some are largely objective in their thinking, and will not trouble their heads with abstract ideas for a very long time. Both types, as they learn to understand more of the character of Jesus, will have a fuller sense of love and strength and discipline in their conception of God.

"*Isn't* it a blessing we've got God?" remarked a three-year-old to me happily, looking up from a floor game. "I don't know *what* we'd do without Him, do you?" This child had her religious ideas growing so naturally along with everything else that it did not seem at all strange to her to remark on them in the middle of a game with her blocks.

An invaluable book for the mother and teacher of little children (from about three years) is Vivyen Bremner's *Thank You, God*. It is followed by *Good and Gay* intended for six to eight years old, and at one time there was a third,

[2] *The Door Opens,* Doubleday & Co. Inc. Copyright 1945. By permission.

Growing Up, all three being books of praise and prayer and religious thinking. The last is illustrated by photographs to go with the poems.

I know of no better first book than *Thank You, God* for the busy parent of today, nor of one better loved by tiny children, especially when it is associated with that quiet time they have with mother or father in the evening. Some parents like to make a book for the child of favorite hymns and little pictures and thoughts. One can of course do both.

Very early, too, the child should have little stories of Jesus, both as a child and as a man. The well-known series of twelve small books, *Bible Books for Small People,* are much loved. They are about the size of the Peter Rabbit books, with the same plan of a few words on each page and a picture opposite it. They enjoy especially Muriel Chambers' *When Jesus was a Boy,* and Mary Entwistle's *Jesus, Friend of Little Children.* Jesus was once a little boy, but he grew to be a man. There is danger in the method used by some people when they teach of Jesus only as a child.

I knew a sensitive, intelligent boy of four years old who had been told only happy stories of the boy Jesus. One day he—Martin—strayed into the cook's bedroom and saw a picture of the Crucifixion on the wall.

"Who's that?" said the child.

"That's Jesus," said Mary, and explained what bad men had done to Him.

"It isn't, it isn't," protested the child. "You are a bad woman and you tell lies. They didn't do that to my Jesus," and he ran from the room in tears to ask his mother about it.

Martin had weeks of disturbed nights and bad dreams. No one knew what to do about it. When Easter came his

friend the minister took him by the hand and let him stand
and listen to the Easter bells. He told the child they were
ringing because Jesus is alive always. Very slowly he was
comforted, and after some weeks he climbed into his
mother's bed one night to tell her a new dream he had had.
He said Jesus had come to see him and had said, "It's
all right, Martin. I'm here and I'm alive. Look at me, here
I am." From that time his serenity returned. I do not
propose to try to analyze this experience, only to suggest
that such suffering in a child's mind might be avoided.

Because of the speed of our time and the lack of domestic help, it is increasingly difficult to find a place in the
day for a quiet time with our children. Mothers say that
just at bedtime—the children's bedtime, I mean—they are
so busy coping with the supper, and perhaps a tired hus-
band, that they are too rushed and weary to give the
children a peaceful time on their own. I know how one
resolves to do certain things with one's children, and how
these plans are slowly pushed into the background if we
do not discipline ourselves continually to form a habit.
I am thinking in particular of the resolve not to let a day
go by without having read at least a few lines of the Bible
together, or of great poetry. One child will have a cold, and
we say, "Tonight we had better not read together because
I don't want you in so-and-so's bedroom." It is very easy
to let it slide altogether.

The ways of every household dictate the best time for a
child to have alone with his mother or father. One busy
mother with several children has a child alone with her
while they wash dishes, and another when she walks over
to the kindergarten to meet her from school. It seems
almost essential to the spiritual and mental health of a

little child to have a few minutes in which to relax with a parent. In homes where there is a bedtime story, this is often the logical time. No matter when, if the child can count on a quiet spell it is of the greatest help in building confidence between him and his parents. As they grow older, the thing that went wrong at school that day, which made them tense and rather cranky when they came home in the afternoon, will be easy to face if they are given a chance to unburden in quietude.

This is the time when children like Martin who are puzzled will ask their questions which they bottle up inside them for fear of ridicule from others. It is the time when the teacher is often guided, because the parent is able to report what is troubling the child and what he needs. After one such talk, the mother of a three-year-old boy met the superintendent of the church school where on the previous day the child had visited the nursery for the first time. The superintendent asked how he had got on. "He loved it," said the mother, "but I do wonder what story they had because he asked me, 'How did the man get off the fence?' Do you have a picture of the Crucifixion there?" She was told that there was not, and moreover it was explained that the story had been of Jesus and the Fishermen, and they had seen a very happy picture, a big one on the wall, they had all chatted about it and seemed to enjoy the story. They decided that at some time the little boy had seen a picture of Jesus nailed to the cross—perhaps at some house where he had visited—and that was his only impression. Now he was puzzled because here was the Man called Jesus sitting in a boat talking to a lot of other people, and how did He get there?

To summarize our beginnings, we see that the child will

find the atmosphere of the home a help or a hindrance to his religious growth: he is affected by the parents' attitude towards each other, towards him, and towards God. Whether the parents consider themselves religious or not does not prevent the child being affected. In extreme cases, where the parents are religiously bigoted and their relation with the child has been unhappy, the child can develop a real antipathy to religion.

We have tried to show the little child that God and His love are round him all the time, that God sent Jesus into the world to reveal Himself, that *Jesus had hard things to do and He Did them.*

Early church experiences are very important, too. Most children like to pay a very short visit to the church on a weekday, with their mother, to stay just a few moments. One little girl who was taken by a grown-up friend said quietly, "I *like* being here." A little later they can go to perhaps the first part of the morning service, for ten minutes or so. And certainly most children love the color and happiness of the special services at Christmas, Easter, and Thanksgiving. In the chapter on church schools we will discuss the pros and cons of the family pew.

I think we shall help our children if, as soon as they are able, we lead them to discover that the word "church" does not necessarily mean the building only. In the liturgy of the Episcopal Church comes the phrase "the whole state of Christ's Church." Wherever the child may worship, it will help him to think of the whole great Christian Family as the church, as well as that particular building in his neighborhood where his own particular section of the world family may go. Let the church be for him People. When the expression "God's House" is used, sometimes in an especially pious tone of voice, the small child quickly builds up the idea that God lives there rather than in other places. I have seen anxious tinies "looking for God" in church, expecting to see Him as a man, while some are so confused that they think the minister is He.

I believe we ought also to try to have the associations that grow around Sunday be the happiest in all the week. Too often it is the day which begins with a great scuffle to get off to church or Sunday School on time. I think we must look to our dispositions on that day with extra care. In some homes there are certain games and books which the children love, and which are kept as a Sunday treat.

We have not thought much up to this point about the appreciation of the world of Nature and that contribution to religious growth. I have not done so purposely, because I think that in both the day school Kindergarten and the Sunday School, nature study is not in danger of being neglected. In many Sunday Schools it is over-emphasized. Many city children, unfortunately, get only an occasional glimpse of wild life in park or garden, unless they can have the happiness of a country vacation or camp. These are so much the poorer, and we must try to help them to discover other means and other roads to satisfy this natural joy which is their birthright. I am thinking of the rather more fortunate child at this moment, the child in the country, or in suburban districts where they have access to these things.

The sense of wonder at out-of-door beauty seems innate in most children, and we can foster their appreciation through the endless possibilities in trees and plants, birds and animals, water creatures and snowflakes. They are part of their discovery of God. But in many Sunday Schools it is overdone, and series of lessons are offered which are neither sound science nor true religion. Their lessons, especially in the earlier years, are apt to be sentimental ones about the dear little birds and butterflies. In spring the children cut out little lambs.

Long before the Junior age is reached the children will begin to ask questions about sex. Parents have lived down the reputation for being flustered and embarrassed at this, and most modern children are no longer tormented with unsatisfied curiosity. But there are still parents who shelve this duty, even in this enlightened age, and children get what facts they want from each other, often crudely. There are those, too, who with an air of conscious virtue hand the children a beautiful modern book on the subject, and feel that their responsibility in this sphere is over.

Recently an otherwise conscientious and highly intelligent mother came to me very distressed because her eleven-year-old son had got himself into difficulties. Inquiry showed that a year ago she gave him an excellent book and told him to read it. Either he never did, or when he tried he was so puzzled and bored that he put it down. Now he had just acquired some exciting and garbled pieces of information from his schoolmates and was in trouble for broadcasting it far and wide.

If parents feel completely inadequate to cope with a child's questions, there is usually a teacher or minister who will help, or a good book read together is a possibility. But because most parents fulfill this duty very well, it seems now not so necessary to remind ourselves of the need for honest teaching and straight thinking about physiological facts, as of the need for reverence. The physical laws are not the whole of the matter. Yeaxlee contends, too, that psychologists like Freud "miss precisely those elements in it which make it genuinely central to primary adolescence and highly significant for religion. These are the elements of the other-regarding propensity and the creative capacity."

The adolescent is much less likely to talk to us, but if as a younger child he has had a good foundation he is able to go forward with clear knowledge and the right attitudes. Usually we can go no farther than that, for the ability of the young adolescent to live with himself—his new self—must be faced alone.

We have seen that the Junior age is the "Is it true?" period. Here we have a few more years before the home retreats somewhat into the background. This is the *realist* period of religious development. We want to satisfy their desire for certainty whenever we can. We need not be afraid of modern research, known as "Higher Criticism," when it comes to Bible study, for we can offer what will be of *lasting* value, as we shall discuss later.

Just as in early childhood fantasy, myth, and legend, as well as some true stories, seem to be the natural food for the child's mind and a real contribution to his religious development, so during the Junior years do they turn to history. This does not mean they no longer appreciate poetry. A poet was once defined as "one who lives on the bridge between the world's contradiction and the soul's imperishable dream, and sets both to music." He will always see further ahead than the scientist. Whether this religious teaching in which he finds his latest knowledge of history and science harmonizing with his earlier religious ideas will come from home or Sunday school, or both, is an individual problem. The child needs it. He must not be left with a pink cloud idea of a God who belongs only to little children. If there is not to be a breakdown of faith as the years pass, his idea of God must grow up along with his wider perception of all things.

This is the time when I think that some of the noblest passages of the Bible and of great poetry should be learned by heart. There comes a time to every man when such a store of treasure is of inestimable value, "when life is too big for our own telling." Great hymns and great prayers come under this heading. In day school he will probably learn some verses by heart. Whether this is real poetry or just tinkling verse depends upon who chooses it for him. The child needs to have his memory stored with lovely things, "hard certain words which could not fail, however much priests might flop and flounder in the pulpit when they spoke with their own human voices . . ." [3] You are thus helping him against those difficult years ahead.

This Junior age is a wonderful one, too, for revealing the unity shared by all great religions. Here the good church school will help, with sound instruction and visits to other churches and synagogues. There is a valuable book,[4] *One God,* by Florence Mary Fitch illustrated by remarkable photographs, which gives the story of the three great religions of this country—the Jewish Way, the Catholic Way, the Protestant Way. It is sound in scholarship, though simple, and will help us to face the battery of questions we must face as time goes on, for the children are certain to meet children who go to churches different from their own.

When the great festivals come round year after year, they bring us unsurpassed opportunities to teach through religious experience and family happiness. The beauty of our faith is

[3] Bruce Marshall, *The World, The Flesh and Father Smith,* p. 91, Houghton Mifflin.
[4] See Chapter Ten.

reinforced, and the maturing life has the chance to re-live that faith at a higher level and with deeper understanding as time goes on. Christmas to the little child is one thing, to the older child another, and so, as life progresses and faith is not destroyed, these great events in the history of the world come with new strength and loveliness.

We all protest at the commercialization of Christmas in the business world, but there is no need for us to let that encroach into our homes. Little children love the color and music of Christmas in the home better than expensive toys. Of this someone wrote,

> Then carols breathe like incense through our furs,
> And magi gifts on jewelled trees arise,
> The Child, crushed faint by elbowing worshippers,
> Behind a thousand counters gasps and dies.[5]

Children like to do for others at this time—to act a play as a special gift to their friends, to make presents, and to sing for them.

Although in the chapter on books we are giving suggestions for Christmas books, we must mention here the very well-known and lovely one, Maud and Miska Petersham's *The Christ Child, as told by Matthew and Luke* which is loved all the year round and especially at Christmas.

Sometimes I feel a little frightened that the constant repetition of the same type of school play at this time will wear off some of the bloom of freshness which should remain. These fears may be unfounded. I think they are less likely to have foundation when there is a change from year to year. But I have seen weary teachers and shivering angels looking disillusioned. In a church setting, and done with reverence,

---

[5] Mary Jenness, "Christmas Shopping."

the whole thing can be offered as a service of worship, and the atmosphere changes. Spontaneous plays done by children in the home come straight from the heart and we have no right to laugh at them, however strange the production. We all know how very tiny children will use all their toy animals in a Nativity scene with the greatest seriousness in the world.

The reserved child relaxes and asks questions. "Why do we celebrate Christmas?" The young child will first think of Christmas as the celebration of the birthday of Jesus. As he grows older we can hope it may be the celebration of the creative power and love of God "who was made Man." Surely this can grow within us to the end of our days. Christmas is not just a time for children, it is a great celebration in the mature religious life. However dark the outside world may be, however much we have failed to use the gift sent us, the light goes on from one generation to another. It is the celebration of joy.

A well-known professor of psychology was recently heard to say that we hear too much about shocks of fear and terror in childhood and their ill effects. "Perhaps," he said, "children have a need for *shocks of blessedness;* their effects on maturity might be correspondingly good." Perhaps at Christmas we might hope for such blessedness. It may come in the beauty of Christmas music, in color, poetry, and formal worship, in hilarity and happiness, and the warmth of reunion. Above all there is the opportunity for service, part of the deepest need of the child's being—"someone to love, something to do." Then if in the stories we tell him we relate the Presentation in the Temple, sometime soon after Christmas, he will perceive once more the idea of being part of the great world family of the Church.

Many parents say they have great difficulty in interpreting

Easter. Could it not be told in some such way as this to little children?

"If someone asked you what you thought were the two happiest days in the year, what would your answer be? Many of us would say 'Christmas and Easter.' We are happy at Christmas because that is Jesus' birthday. At Easter we are happy because that is when His first friends found out that Jesus is with us always and nothing can take Him away from us. How do we know? One way we are sure is because of what happened on the very first Easter morning." It might be told as follows:

"The Friday before Easter Day was a sad one. You know about that. Some people hated Him because He told them the truth, and they killed Him. You can imagine how dreadfully sad His friends were. Some of them had been with Him for three years, going up and down the country with Him as He taught and worked, making sick people well, and sad ones happy. He had been their Teacher too, and they had walked and talked and gone to their church together (you remember it was called a synagogue), and we think they often ate their food out of doors, He and His friends. On Good Friday they thought He had been taken from them forever, and they were like lost children, they just didn't know what to do next.

"Something happened on Easter morning to show His friends He was with them just the same. Very early, before it was light, some women who were Jesus' friends went to a beautiful garden. They saw a man standing there whom they thought was the gardener. One of the women, whose name was Mary Magdalene, spoke to him. When he answered with her name, 'Mary' she realized it was Jesus. She said, 'Master,' and the women were so full of joy that they ran to tell his other friends. Instead of feeling lonely they were happy and excited. They knew Jesus was stronger than Death.

"In the Bible we can read many stories of how Jesus came back to His friends. One of the loveliest happened on Easter Sunday, a little later in the day. Two men were walking to a place called Emmaus, feeling very miserable, just as Mary Magdalene had done. While they were talking they suddenly realized there was another man walking along with them.

" 'Why are you so unhappy?' said the stranger, 'what is it you are talking about that makes you so sad?'

"They were very puzzled, and they said, 'You must have come from a long way off. Haven't you heard of what's been happening in the last few days? Haven't you heard of Jesus of Nazareth?'

"And the stranger said, 'Tell me about it.' So the two men told him all about Jesus, and how they had gone to the garden that morning after the women had seen Him, but they couldn't find Him.

"They walked along together until evening, until they came to the village, and they asked the stranger to have supper with them. At supper the stranger said Grace for them, and as they began to eat they understood it was Jesus, and that they had spent all that time with Him without knowing. They were so happy, that like the women in the garden they ran off at once, all the way back to the city, to tell the others. I think you would have wanted to do that.

"So when Easter comes, with the birds and sunshine, and all the world waking up after its winter sleep, we remember all over again that nothing can take Jesus away from us, He is with us forever, just as He was with His first friends."

However excellent the teacher, in day school or church school, the younger child is unlikely to reveal his deeper questionings in the same way as he will to an understanding parent. We have been rightly called the mediators of reality, and we have seen that the parent-child relationship is one of the elements of religion. It is our solemn duty to make this relationship happy, to feed the child's expanding life, not only with all the obvious material and body-building things in which we are so much less likely to fail, but with some of the world's store of fantasy and legend and poetry, together with his Bible teaching, food for his perception of God; history and science; the interpretation of other faiths; opportunities for loving and serving.

Heaven help us if we miss, for in the next few years he will be trying his wings in the world; he will meet the skeptic and the cynic. Shall we have given him some straight truth to fight with?

Children and Religion

HELPFUL BOOKS FOR TEACHERS AND PARENTS OF YOUNGER CHILDREN

WILLIAMS, JOHN G., *Worship and the Modern Child,* Macmillan

WHITCOMB, DOROTHY, *Answers to a Child,* Mowbray, available at Morehouse

WYNN, J. C., *How Christian Parents Face Family Problems,* Westminster

PROCTOR, ANNE, *The Christian Household,* Longmans

WHEATCROFT, ANITA, *Preface for Parents,* Seabury. For expectant parents

ROORBACK, R., *Religion in the Kindergarten,* Harper

WILKINSON, FLORENCE, *Growing up in Christ,* Seabury

NOT SPECIFICALLY RELIGIOUS

GRUENBERG, S., *The Parents' Guide to the Everyday Problems of Boys and Girls,* Random House

JOHNSON, JUNE, *Home Play for the Preschool Child,* Harper

JOHNSON, JUNE, *838 Ways to Amuse a Child,* (6–8 yrs.), Harpers

PLAY-EQUIPMENT FOR YOUNG CHILDREN

Community Playthings, Rifton, N.Y. Write for their leaflet, "Play Equipment and Your Church Preschool." (Catalog also available)

FURTHER HELP

TOBEY, K. M., *The Church Plans for Kindergarten Children,* Westminster

HERON, F. D., *Kathy Ann, Kindergartner,* Abingdon. (A child's impressions of Sunday School)

CHAPTER FOUR

Adolescence

Let not your souls be smothered out before
They do quaint deeds and fully flaunt their pride.
It is the world's one crime its babes grow dull,
Its poor are ox-like, limp, and leaden-eyed.

Not that they starve, but starve so dreamlessly,
Not that they sow, but that they seldom reap;
Not that they serve, but have no gods to serve,
Not that they die, but that they die like sheep.

—VACHEL LINDSAY, "The Leaden-Eyed"

Just as there is an urgency about the first two stages of human life and its religious development—an urgency that demands first the opportunity for the slow perception of God through experience, then the harmonizing of the earlier ideas with new knowledge of history and science, so there is an even greater urgency about the adolescent years, for, as has been said, many things are to be done at this time or not at all. Meanwhile parents have to stand in the background and let other influences, which we hope will be the right ones, come to their aid.

Some learned people have tried to be almost diagrammatic in their theories on just how to classify the development of adolescents, even going so far as to indicate the exact age at which various characteristics will appear, in boys and in girls. It is surely a nearer proximation of the truth to observe that in different personalities there will be a varying degree of turmoil, in some there will be apparently little or none. Adolescent young people are, as we discussed in Chapter Two, awakening on the emotional and on the intellectual side, they are being born into a newly-discovered world. The horizon of the entire universe has for them enlarged and changed.

Professor J. B. Pratt in the chapter on this age in his book, *The Religious Consciousness,* reminds us that it is "the flowering time for religion—it is not the time of fruitage, that comes later on." Later he says, "Youth is the time for hailing the vision and coming to love the light, the religious task of the great middle years is to live and act in the light that has been seen." [1]

Adolescence is like the opening of a door into a world much bigger and more beautiful than anything contemplated before; but it is also the entry into a sphere of greater dangers, perhaps the worst of these being disillusionment and loss of faith. The flame kindled in childhood will either grow stronger or become so dim as to be only a flicker. The headmaster of a famous school, if ever he finds himself feeling very gratified at the success of his methods, looks at one older boy after another, and asks himself, "Has he fulfilled the promise of the nursery?" To save this promise, he contends, is the central problem of education. He says many boys do not *grow* up into adult life, they age into it. I believe that a satisfying religious life can prevent this.

John Bunyan's *Pilgrim's Progress* is not really out of date, our adolescent will meet nearly all the same people in his

[1] P. 120, Macmillan. Copyright 1920. By permission.

pilgrimage. C. S. Lewis, in his *Pilgrim's Regress,* shows us some of the characters in a new guise, and we can invent a good many other names for those the young people must meet as they go along. Some thinkers believe that the period of doubt is almost inevitable, and it is true that some adolescents go through a period of doubting almost everything, and even go so far as to contend that faith is something you have to lose before it can be regained as a personal possession. Unfortunately the second stage is not always reached.

We are faced, then, with three types: 1. Those who had really creative experiences and good instruction in childhood, whether by precept or example, and they are ready to go forward to look for more. 2. Those who had neither of these advantages, and are now looking vaguely for some nameless desire. 3. Those who had a religious interest in childhood, but finding it would not wear well, cast it off as useless.

For the first we hope to go on providing those things which his full development demands. The second and third will have to retrace their steps, either forced by circumstances as the years go on, or helped now by wise adults, and coming into contact with other young people who are looking for the same thing. In several states religious conferences are held for boys and girls of fourteen and over, chosen from various schools. They live in a community life for a week or so, and have the valuable experience of corporate worship; they have discussion groups led by fine men and women who are working in different fields, and who are up against the practical problems of today; and they have some outdoor life. These conferences are splendid because the serious-minded do not imagine themselves to be unique and are not afraid to air their views: they find themselves in a crowd of people looking for the same thing, and are not ashamed to own it; they find these people heathy-minded youngsters like themselves, fond of play and pretty clothes, and athletics. Of a speaker at one of these conferences, I heard a typical modern girl say, "He is wise, but you feel he is seeking, just as we are." These young crusaders know what it feels like to come down from the mountain-top and to mix with those who measure the good of a thing only by the number of those who take part in it.

Some parents are afraid of highly emotional experiences at conferences of this kind giving an artificial and fleeting enthusiasm. My personal experience has been that of seeing the love of fun and the fear of sentimentality, which are surely characteristics of modern youth, keep the balance, and there is no morbid excitement. The attitude is rather, "The world is in a bad way. What would happen if we tried to carry out the teachings of Christianity?" The hardest time for those who have attended conferences is when they must come down from the mountain-top and live with the heathen they used to be. Then comes the struggle to test out their new vision and try to find reality.

The professional teacher can at this time become the stabilizing factor in adolescence. He is able to be detached from the child's life, and the child has not the involved emotional ties he has with his parents. Here is the time, too, when vocational interests begin to grow. Some fortunate young people discover these very early and never depart from them, but others, as we all know, wander aimlessly and eventually take the wrong line. Schools are on the whole too much withdrawn from the world, and this has tended to make it harder for children to choose their vocations. In college many find what they need, but many do not go to college, and have to make a choice when they leave High School. It helps young people if they can see the specialist in various fields contributing his part to the great stream of life, and to see it in relation to the whole, discovering the struggle and devotion which lie behind the life of every true craftsman, artist, scholar and scientist. If either parents or teachers—or perhaps both—will give the young people a chance to meet men and women at their jobs, they will see that in order to reach a goal, whether of physical or mental achievement, anyone will have to undergo a certain amount of self-discipline and a giving-up of other things.

He will see his chosen career either as a means of "getting on" and making money, or as his particular contribution to society—part of the creative spirit at work in the world. Our job as parents is the same as that of his teachers: to give him as many experiences as possible. Too often he is given a smattering of many subjects and no contact with active life. But we must work together. We teach in school or church school that the Kingdom of God must come first while the world praises the man who makes most money and lives most comfortably; the church teaches that the world is ruled by one great loving force, the outer world flouts authority and admires the man who can best evade its demands. The young are confused.

The need for an awakening was demonstrated only too clearly at a kindergarten training college of repute; recently, at a meeting of three hundred students, only three thought religious education of any importance—so materialistic have we become. I cannot believe that this would have been the case if they had been brought into contact with those who could in their lives and personalities demonstrate a living faith, and represent what we have described before: religion in *activity*. Most young people today never have a chance to find out what religion is. We adults must try to keep ourselves informed of the rapid trends of today—internationally, politically, religiously, socially—and where we ourselves are not able to interpret, it is our bounden duty to bring our children to those who can.

We have seen that from childhood upwards we should also try to give our children opportunities to serve. Christianity teaches that a power for good lies behind this world. Our children are more likely to perceive this if through service they may identify themselves with that power; we must try to give them the experience of becoming a part of it, as early as possible. We have seen that religious instruction cannot reveal this, the children must know it through experiences in their own lives. The need is so deep in the child's nature that he will almost certainly find something for himself. We want to lead him to find a *worthy* cause, to which he may bring his vitality and enthusiasm. What is likely, in this modern world, to influence these potentialities besides the religious life that has gone before? If from childhood upward we have nurtured this desire for "something to love and something to do," and if he has come up against all sorts and conditions of men, he will be more likely to sense the need he can fill. To some the decision to follow a certain vocation will come as a veritable call of God—but only, alas, to the fortunate few. Whether the foundations beneath our children are weak or strong, they must learn to recognize the subtle forces which will lie in wait for them all their days: the first of these is propaganda—or, as it is more delicately put, "the technique of persuasion."

The influences of propaganda will play upon our children whatever we do, so obviously their only defense is to be able to recognize them and to bring a critical faculty to bear upon them; moreover, if a sense of humor is a sense of proportion, they will need that, too. Once their life-work is discerned and themselves dedicated to it, the danger is less: it is in the precarious choosing time beforehand that their energy may be seduced into the wrong channels.

As we have previously seen, the influences of propaganda beat upon the modern child from the cradle. From time to time, the ideas it is trying to convey will change, but the machine remains the same: the movies, television, the radio, the public press, cheap books and high-powered advertising are all part of it. Hitler understood it and expounded his theories with great frankness in *Mein Kampf;* any modern school of advertising knows the same technique. You are made to believe what the State wants you to believe, to follow what it wants you to follow, to buy what commerce ordains you shall buy, a receptive emotional condition has been previously induced in you. The danger which interests us especially in our study of the development of a young religious life is that adolescence is the normal crusading time, and the adolescent therefore particularly prone to follow. "The technique of persuasion" treats you as a very fine specimen of human nature, and is in itself cloaked in virtue ("distinctive gowns for ladies of good taste"); actually it is based on a very low idea of the individual, and is a denial of the Christian doctrine of personality.

The personal effort needed to sift and select and formulate these beliefs is the opposite to the passive condition of mind that makes fertile ground for the slow but constant infiltration of ideas brought to us by propaganda. Emotional attitudes *without understanding* are what we must avoid for the child if we are to keep the integrity of his spirit, for with adolescence comes the time for personal choice.

We have seen the parodied proverb which reads, "When

religion is thrust out by the door it comes in again by the window." Here are our adolescents at the very point when they will adopt some great enthusiasm, and if it comes in at the window in the form of some devotion to a political movement, we must not be surprised if it dominates their whole life. In early adolescence the usual hero worship and gang spirit has been nourished, and those who have observed the effects as the young person grows into such movements say that they give themselves with a religious devotion and complete self-surrender.

To summarize what we have seen so far: we find ourselves realizing the urgent need to have the idealism and energy of adolescents directed into the right channels, and also to have them choose wisely in their vocation. At the same time we find it necessary to retreat into the background and let the professional teacher and others come forward, especially those engaged in a wide variety of occupations and professions. We want them to help the young person to creative experience without superimposing ideas, so that he develops the power to make wise personal choice. We want him to understand the technique of the propaganda which will always beset him. We want him to have opportunities for service, without which he cannot have a deeper religious experience.

Having these ideals in mind, let us look with complete honesty at the things lying in the path of the average adolescent today, and as we do so we should remember that above all he wants to stand well with the group, exclusion from it is something he can rarely bear to contemplate. Therefore he is often, consciously or unconsciously, trying to get rid of a certain moral sensitiveness, because he wants to stand well with his peers. We know, too, that he finds himself as a little child for the second time—he has to find himself all over again in relation to his environment, and also in relation to the community.

Almost certainly your adolescent will enjoy the movies. He is going through a time of emotional upheaval, and will find through them much vicarious enjoyment. Most adolescents like radios and popular music. They are in varying degrees interested in such columns in newspapers and magazines as "boy meets girl." Clothes are of great significance, and if possible the teen-agers must dress like everyone else in their age-group, for this is the period of self-consciousness and age-consciousness. If adventurous they may want to try smoking and other fads. Because of their tendency to continue hero-worship they fall in love with movie stars. Strangely enough, they are also ready for very serious religious discussions.

The recent thoughtful discussions among serious-minded people who are anxious to help teen-agers have revolved round the question, "What should the church do?" And the answer seems to be, "Study local situations and provide the opportunities and activities young people need in the name of Christianity. Give them what they need for a completely rounded life."

We do not wish to over-emphasize the group aspects of the adolescent problem, but since the young people of this age are almost certain to "gang together," a certain amount of group activity, through home, church, and school seems essential. We must not lose sight of the fact that they also need some time alone, just as younger children do. Nearly all young people like to have a room or a place where they can face their problems in solitude. This is unfortunately not possible for each one of them, and so frequently depends on their financial position. Some put "love of aloneness" as one of the chief characteristics of this age, together with "love of enterprise" and "love of skill."

The story is told of a boy who ran away from a pioneer school in Europe which was said to be full of a "joyous restlessness." He and a friend ran way across the Alps and had great adventures. The older boy was punished by the loss of his holidays, and after work one day he was found to be doing a most remarkable piece of sculpture, the figure of a "tired but determined runner by the wayside." When he was asked why he had never done work like that before, he said "I can only do such things when I am sad, and I have had no opportunity to be sad."

This is no place for a detailed account of Young People's Fellowships and the many other organizations formed to help young people. Local situations demand different methods. Some fellowships are merely dating opportunities; others are doing strong and splendid work. The standards by which we live, even in a few years, have changed. Youth needs good counselors, and in districts where the best work is being done, it comes about naturally that when the programs become youth-centered, the adults give themselves in many ways, growing along with the young people, and with them facing the problems of the world, the community, and the individual. It is of no use pulling the wool over our eyes. Those who counsel youth today must have great courage and be ready to face difficulties that would have floored our ancestors. What have we to say to these young people who are being jeered at in no uncertain terms for their interest in Christianity, and can we in our own lives demonstrate a quality of life and achievement which will make them want to resolve one of their worst tensions—the desire to stand well with their friends, and the pull in the other direction, towards a higher level of good?

Randolph C. Miller analyzes the position in an article called "Bobby-Sox Religion." He says, "It is hard to realize that the 'bobby-sox' crowd . . . , has serious religious problems. For some in the older generation, modern jazz does not appear to be a new form of art; and improvising on the theme of Tiger Rag . . . does not seem like music appreciation. . . . Yet these same youngsters will enjoy a talk by a missionary from China or a cadet-chaplain in the navy. And they will seek counsel and plan to be baptized with utmost seriousness. Almost all of these factors can be observed at a summer Church Conference, which is where the more fortunate youngsters are guided by the best informed church leaders in seeking answers to their questions.

"Ultimately, it is the youngsters themselves who solve their problem, resolve their conflicts, and release their tensions. The responsibility of adults is to see that they move in the right direction, have resources for wide choices, and develop their own potentialities in the service of God. . . . The adults are the trustees of a great tradition." [2]

The cynic will tell you that it is quite impossible for the world to progress, because we do not start where the previous generation left off, we will not listen to them, and since experience is the only sure teacher, we make the same mistakes over again. But surely if the new generation can be guided by those who put God first, it is possible to point the way. We cannot be sure that they will follow it, but the least we can do is to give them a chance. For when unhappiness comes to young people, whether as a fleeting thing or real tragedy,

[2] "Bobby-Sox Religion" *Religious Education,* March–April, 1946.

those who are close to them will testify that the invariable cry is, "Why didn't somebody tell me? If only I'd known, this need not have happened."

Let us see to it that through Bible study and religious opportunity adolescents have some idea of the vast sweep of religious thought and action through the ages. We will let him taste—socially, artistically, intellectually—of the trends of our time, so that having tasted one value after another, he can evaluate for himself, and having seen the vision, desire above all things to dedicate himself to the final good, the creative power of God working in the universe today.

Adolescence

BOOKS ON HELPING ADOLESCENTS

CHAPLIN, DORA P., *We Want to Know,* Morehouse. For Young People, also for adults who live and work with them

BARUCH, DOROTHY W., *How to Live with Your Teen-ager,* McGraw-Hill

JONES, G. CURTIS, *Parents Deserve to Know,* Macmillan

GALLAGHER, J. R. and HARRIS, H. I., *Emotional Problems of Adolescents,* Oxford

SALISBURY, HARRISON, *This Shook-up Generation,* Harper

WITTENBERG, RUDOLPH M., *Adolescence and Discipline: A Mental Hygiene Primer,* Association Press

For the ⎰ DUVALL, EVELYN M., *The Facts of Life and Love for Teen-*
young ⎬ *agers,* Association Press
people ⎱ DUVALL, EVELYN M., *The Art of Dating,* Association Press

The best High School magazine for young people is called *Hi-way,* and is published by The Westminster Press, Witherspoon Building, Philadelphia, Pa.

CHAPTER FIVE

Prayer

Grant, O Lord, that our petitions may always be for those things
that may fit us to please Thee, and not for such as may be the
fittest to please ourselves; and for an accumulation of blessings,
so influence our souls with Thy Divine Spirit, that Thy will may
ever be our pleasure; through Jesus Christ our Lord. Amen.

—CHARLES HOW, 1661

There will always be many definitions of prayer. One dictionary defines it as a "solemn request to God or object of worship," whereas worship is explained as "paying religious homage to." In the minds of many people, just as to the author of the dictionary, prayer is just "a request." This is no place for quibbling over the problems of semantics, but we should have some idea of what we mean by prayer.

To avoid confusion, let us in this chapter regard prayer and worship as synonymous, and before we bring great ideas to bear upon the level of a child's worship, let us look at a few more definitions.

Prayer has been described as the regarding of today in relation to Eternity. It has been called the medium of highest beauty; the celebration of life. Again, I once heard a preacher describe prayer as the time when the spirit turns to the Father of the spirit, and thinks God's thoughts after Him, trying not to alter His plan, but to make His plan ours. This makes prayer a way of living in God.

The idea of prayer as a way of living in God is perhaps a little nearer what we are looking for. The first prayer of a little child should be the experience of a short time of thinking, loving, enjoying—with God. This is a preparation for prayer as contemplation. The road to mature communion with God calls for a slow-footed journey; because worship is an activity of the soul, we must learn to let activity proceed at its own pace.

Though we are primarily concerned with setting the young child on the right path, we must also consider those whose prayer life has been damaged or destroyed. Experience shows that many little children whose religious life unfolds naturally seem to have, in some unfathomable way, a perception through which the character of Jesus is already half-knowledge, as though, when you teach, you are only introducing two dear friends already known to each other. Many parents testify to this experience.

We must above all remember that the kind of worship offered, whether by young or old, will depend on the person's belief in *God*. If the grown-ups have misled the child into thinking of God as a severe personage dwelling "above the bright blue sky," ministered to by a company of well-behaved cherubs, and handing out reward or punishment—the child will naturally cling to that conception, and try to further his own little petitions as a matter of course. If, on the other hand, God is regarded as a vague spirit or principle, the child will feel lost, and we can sympathize with the one who cried in the dark and pleaded for "a God with a face." There is a prayer sometimes used in churches which asks that we be not misled into thinking of God as so familiar that we know *all* of Him, or so remote that we can never find Him.

Ideas which to our adult minds present great difficulties are sometimes much easier for a child to absorb. For example, invisibility does not usually trouble him, although one meets a few children who have been frightened by the idea of an unseen presence. Most children have their "pretend friends," and the step from pretence to reality is not a long one. They can also grasp a difference of space and time: the idea that "one day is with the Lord as a thousand years and a thousand years as one day" can be learned very early. It is also very important to avoid the idea that God is more in one place than another. We shall touch on this question in connection with the church.

We have already referred briefly to a psychologist's attitude to religious life—that is, the attitude of those who contend that the religious life alone can meet the needs of growing minds and mature personality. I think we agreed that we cannot escape from this fact. We also saw that our unconscious influence on the lives of the children we teach is incalculable. Now we have to meet the often-misused word "mysticism." Many people have the notion that mysticism means seances, or visions of an unhealthy nature, and are therefore rightly on the defensive when it is mentioned. We are concerned here with the mystic life only in the sense of its being a basic need of the human soul, a normal thing, and not in its manifestation in extreme forms.

Professor J. B. Pratt goes into the subject in much detail, especially in the chapter, "The Belief in a God," [1] where he shows mysticism in proportion to the other essentials of a

[1] *The Religious Consciousness*, p. 479.

well-founded faith. He ends on this note: "In our safe and sane and sober fear of emotionalism and sentimentality, we seem to disown the spiritual nature *which is part of our human heritage.* Even social justice and college settlements and industrial democracy and international amity are not enough to satisfy the full warm life of the soul. The soul needs a larger draft of air, a less circumscribed horizon, than even these excellent things can give. It needs a chance for spreading its wings, for looking beyond itself, beyond the immediate environment, and for quiet inner growth, which is best found in that group of somewhat indefinite but very real experiences —aspiration, insight, contemplation—which may well be called 'the mystic life.' "

If we could rid ourselves of the idea that the mystic life is an abnormality, we should see it, unexpressed in words, in the lives of some of the more radiant and dynamic personalities we meet. These heightened lives may be lived all unconsciously in the presence of God. The only mystics are not those who are articulate, and have been able to leave their experiences expressed in literature.

If we hope to bring our very young children into touch with these sources of power, we must never lose sight of the need for *experiences* rather than explanations. One mother recalls that she felt it was time to talk to her three-year-old about God. She said one evening at bath-time, "Now, dear, I think the time has come for us to talk about God."

"Who's God?" asked the child.

"Well," said the mother, fumbling. "He gave you all the birds and flowers and trees and everything you see."

"Why did He?" said the young philosopher.

"Because he thought you'd like them," explained his mother.

"Well, I don't," replied the child thoughtfully.

This reaction was unexpected, but I think the mother asked for it. How our children hate the saccharine voice and the tense moments of imposed instruction!

Think of a better way. The little child's first experience of prayer may well come to him as suggested in Chapter Three, when the sight of a parent kneeling by his bed may call forth a feeling of love and reverence to the One to Whom the prayers are said. The child usually wants to share in this friendship, and all the ways are slowly opened for his questioning. "Who are you talking to?" "Where is God?" "What does He look like?" and so on. Usually he wants to "say his prayers," too. I sometimes wish we could drop that expression, for *saying one's prayers* is not the same as *praying*. Although we want to establish the habit of prayer, we do not want it to be on the same level as the habit of brushing the teeth before going to bed. There is a danger of slipping into well-worn grooves and letting these childhood prayers become a convention or plaything. We have seen too often the expression of adoring sentimentality on the face of a relative, while "Johnnie says his prayers like a good boy." And how very good he feels. We have every right to respect the prayer life of a child, not drag it into the region of nursery rhymes.

Our own prayer habits, as we have seen, will influence the child's. If we are "in love with God" he will catch some of our enthusiasm if it is deep and real. A simple example of this is in story telling. We know how it is impossible to convey the humor or pathos of a story unless we feel it and see it ourselves.

The instinct for worship seems to be in every child, but it does not develop on the same lines, nor at the same rate. In the same family you will find your objective child, and your child to whom the inner life is from the beginning an integral part of his existence. We must be careful to value these different types, and not to hurry the development of any. Each has his place and his work to do. Your objective child may grow up to be the man who is busy living a Christian life and takes no time to talk about it. The other child needs to put his vision into activity. The objective child will be in awe of God through the things in which He reveals His strength in the world of things seen. If he is forced he will refuse to pray at all. Nearly every child you deal with will ask you why he cannot see God. The illustration of the unseen work of a wind blowing usually helps—the idea of a Power we know is there, we can see what the wind does, as the trees sway and the leaves move, but not the wind itself.

Above all try to have the early religious experiences *happy,* so that the name God is associated with joyful things. At bedtime he finds himself with his father or mother, they are going to speak to God together, and share with Him some of the good things that have happened during the day; or perhaps they are going to look at a picture, or listen to some music that is emotionally quiet and satisfying. Or they may read together, not necessarily a story that is formally religious. These times can be the high spot of the child's day, and into them the thought of God becomes interwoven. We can be careful always not to isolate them from the experiences of everyday life, we want to talk over the events of the day together. We must not have a dividing line between this special time we give to God and our daily life, the same line of demarcation which can fall between a pious Sunday and a materialistic Monday.

Because of the desire to share happiness, a child's first spoken prayer is usually one of gratitude. One early prayer

I heard ran like this: "Oh thank you, God, for our muddy garden and my Sister Baby and the lovely spiders. I want to be a Good Big Girl. Amen."

When I visited at Christ Church, Hyde Park, Massachusetts, I found they were about to hold a Children's Day of Prayer. The church was to remain open all one Saturday for the children, from the Second grade through High School age, to go in and say the prayers they had written anonymously and handed to their teachers. They could go at any time and pray in any part of the church they chose. The following is a selection from the children's prayers that were kindly sent to me by the Rector; they throw some light on how our children like to pray:

"Dear Lord, Bless the poor children in Europe, help the more fortunate countries to spare food to help these starving children. Help also O God, the leaders of various countries to see that peace is much better than war. Amen."

"Almighty God who watched over people who are in trouble or sick, please watch over all mothers who may be sick and lonesome, through Jesus Christ our Lord. Amen."

"O merciful God, Giver of life, health and happiness, make thy people happy and kind hearted. Through Jesus Christ Our Lord. Amen."

"Lord, forgive my sins that I have committed; Help me to do the things that are right, and to forget the wrong and evil. I will help Thee Lord maker of earth in all ways. Amen."

"Dear Lord in heaven, help us to know thee better every day and to realize the great meaning you have in our lives.

64

Help us to know and appreciate the beauty of nature and the things you have created. Give us strength to understand and do good; make us humble before thee. Lord make us better people by helping others, help those who are sick and in need of spiritual guidance. Oh heavenly Father, help us to know right from wrong by knowing Thee. Amen."

"Oh Lord, my trust is in thy mercy and my heart is joyful in thy salvation. Dear Father I shall try all the days of my life to follow thy commandments, Oh, take care of us Lord all the days of our life, Do not let me follow evil. Dear Lord I am grateful and thankful for the help of thy good hand. Amen."

"Our Father who art in heaven, blessed be thy name. The Lord is great and helpful not only to me but to others everywhere. Help me to do what God says. Help me in school if I try. Give us time to correct the wrongs we have done, and help us to do the things we have forgotten. We must help others before God will help us. Help us to do things right. We are truly grateful for the things God does for us. Amen."

Children will vary very much, according to their powers of expression and their own wishes, as to when they want to use their own words in prayer. Others will choose to use them from the very beginning, rejecting the words of other people, and talking to God as naturally as to another friend. A "thanking book" much loved from about three years old is Harold Burdekin's *A Child's Grace*. It is related to the child's daily experience, and each verse is illustrated by a big photograph of familiar things. Other recent books have appeared in which prayers are illustrated by well-known artists.

There is much controversy over the question of grace before meals. Some argue that it is artificial to be more grateful for food than for any other of God's gifts which happen to have been part of the day. But we forget God so often that surely if grace can be a short recollection of Him when we gather as a family, it would be the good use of an opportunity only too rare in our crowded days. If we make it a family custom, let us avoid the stereotyped. Many of us are haunted by recollections of little children muttering, "Thank-God-for-my-good-dinner-Amen-please-now-mother-may-I-get-down-from-the-table?"

The verse:

> All good gifts around us
> Are sent from heaven above;
> Then thank the Lord, O thank the Lord,
> For all His love

is nearer a comprehensive idea of thankfulness than the ones confined to the blessing of food only.

Parents will be interested in *A Little Book of Singing Graces,* collected by Jeanette Perkins Brown.

The very tiny child may say:

> God is loving,
> God is good,
> And we thank Him
> For this food.

Thanking God, and sharing with God, we have seen seem to go together naturally. The child brings to God what he likes best and offers it. The heart of true prayer is a spirit of love for God, and the habit of bringing to Him what we like best is a real experience of prayer, the beginning of the time when the instinct for prayer turns into friendship with God.

Recently, talking to a group of about six little girls eleven years old whom I had known for several years, we fell into a discussion of the times when they felt God closest to them. They put their ideas together after a time and made a thanksgiving prayer:

> "We thank Thee for the night and day, stars that light the way, and all the lovely things we see and know. We thank Thee for the beauty of mountains and valleys, rocks and streams, colors that make us happy, ripe harvests and harvesting. We thank Thee for the gentleness of little animals.
>
> "We are thankful we can be close to Thee when we are sad or happy, alone or being friendly, in church or school, when we sleep or play, when we are afraid or when we are glad, and when we see little children.
>
> "When we are forgiven our hearts are full of thanks, when we are forgiving and making others happy; and when we read of Thee, O Lord.
>
> "Without Thee there would be no world. Amen."

Then come prayers of *Petition*. These "asking" prayers are of two kinds, personal requests, and requests made for others, which we call intercession. They are both fraught with dangers and can raise any number of theological questions. Far into maturity comes the time when we can say with the Indian mystic, "ever Thou hast upheld me with wise refusals."

I once knew an intense little girl of six who listened to a sermon on "Ask, and ye shall receive," which she took literally. Her misguided parents told me with pride that she had spent nearly two hours on her knees asking that her favorite doll should get up and walk round the room. What effect would such a lack of an "answer" to prayer have on the faith of a little child?

An eleven-year-old recently said to me very happily, "I've discovered God does answer prayers, though not always the way you expect." And I was reminded of a boy of the same age who wanted a bicycle for Christmas. He prayed earnestly for it, at the behest of one of his devout aunts. Christmas came, and there was no bicycle. The aunt said to the child in a very sentimental voice, "I'm so sorry, dear, God did not answer your prayer"; to which the boy replied, "But he did. He said No, I couldn't have it."

If we can only qualify our petitions with, "Thy will be done," or "If it be Thy will," not trying to change God's plan for our lives, but making His plan ours in the self-surrender of religious maturity, on what a different plane do we speak to Him! Many thoughtful people teaching young people recommend that very little stress should be laid upon prayer as petition until we have helped the child to build part of the Father and Son relationship with God, by enlarging his idea of the Father. A child knows his earthly parents do not always give him what he wants.

In another way confusion comes to the child when he has made secret requests to God about, let us say, the weather, and they have in his opinion been answered for the express purpose of allowing him to go to a ball game. This has been aptly described as letting a child consider himself to be "assistant manager of the Universe."

The request for virtue is yet another snare. We may ask for strength or for grace, but the request that God shall *make us good* is apt to bring the same disillusionment as to the child with the doll—"I asked God to make me good, and He didn't." Some mothers with an honest conviction help the children to see that, if we *try*, God will help us on the last lap, just as when we lend a hand with a complicated snow suit, but only after we have seen them try it first alone.

Asking for others is petition at a higher level. It is a long hard way to the stage when we believe that our love, through God, can be carried to a sick and suffering world. Some people, like the little child we have just considered, prefer to ask for grace to do something about it. I believe that the strenuous creative love of a mature life is a force of comfort to those who need it. But for a little child to ask God to make a beloved grandmother well again, and to have it denied, is to come again to the loss of faith that overtook the child with the doll. But prayers of intercession rightly directed can help the growing mind to reach beyond itself to the family, the church, the whole world.

We must not confuse true intercession with the lazy method of good-night prayers which are just a string of "God bless so-and-so," *ad infinitum,* an ancient method of postponing bedtime as late as possible, and known to all. Honest children eventually get weary of this farce. Bless is a lazy word, and most children do not know what they mean by it. I once heard a sturdy small boy, who had been taught to "say his prayers" rather than to pray, get off his knees one night in desperation, saying, "You can all God-bless yourselves tonight, for I'm tired."

Repentance is yet another form of prayer. In the little book, *Thank you, God,* a form of repentant prayer is suggested. It is for the mother to think through and use only if she is sure the child is ready for it. How often is a child really sorry for what he has done? We frequently hear, "You shall not do so-

and-so until you have said you are sorry," and the child says, "I'm sorry" as a talisman to get himself back into the good graces of the grown-ups.

I am reminded of the true story of a three-year-old girl disobediently jumping into puddles, splashing her best clothes and looking back at her escort saying, "I'm sorry I jumped into that puddle. But I'm sorry I'm just going to jump into another puddle." That child was honest. We have agreed that in the building of a religious life we want to avoid hypocrisy. Children, who come to church school for the first time at the age of ten or so, often reveal to us the idea of God as a Man with a big stick Who sees all they do and will punish them. By this time their attitude is one of defiance: parents have held this idea of God over them, they have already misbehaved a good deal and the Man with the big stick has done nothing about it.

If we remind ourselves constantly that *saying* we are sorry is not the same as *being* sorry, we may help the child prepare for the mature undertaking of repentance. The parable of the Lost Sheep helps them. They understand that God is like the shepherd who looked for the lamb who ran away, and that when we run away from Him, His love calls to us to come back. When you talk it over with them afterwards they always see the folly of saying you are sorry and not doing anything about it. "You've got to *try*," they will tell you, in their logical way. Very few modern children from happy homes think that God never loves you again if you are bad, but this is not true where a policeman God has been inflicted on them.

The average church school no longer preaches hell-fire and eternal punishment. I sometimes wonder if we err the other way. Are we afraid to use the word "sin" any more?

For fear of doing harm, I think we do not emphasize the justice of God enough, so that a shallow, lukewarm goodness emerges from our teaching. The Christian way is hard, we had better see that from the first. When we sin, we are disloyal to God, and we are truly repentant only when we are willing to give up what separates us from Him, and to rededicate ourselves.

Real repentance, in a mature sense, goes through three phases—first comes the realization of an ideal as yet unattained, then the wish to reach it, finally the summoning of strength to reach that ideal, which results in a change of mind. The child may be helped to this by discussing what happened. Supposing there has been a quarrel. If he can see that neither he nor Mary were right, he will be nearer real penitence than the uttering of a set of formal words can bring him. His repentance may take the form of action, he may want to do something about it. If he also, spontaneously, wants to "tell God about it," he is ready for prayers of repentance, and not before.

Sometimes prayer-time can be a talk with our children; or, as we have seen, the reading of poetry or a story. Or you can make together a litany of things that have happened during the day, or a thinking prayer, as the other children did. At these times the child will sometimes want to talk about his world as it is being revealed to him, and of his fears and battles, even of his anger. As the years go on, and the injustice and misery of our civilization become manifest, he may grow more angry and more bewildered. Only if you can keep the vision of the perfection of God before him will he be able to continue to pray. Anger at sorrow and sin must not be the end, for it may lead to egoism, and despair. If you can hold him to the sight of God made Man in Jesus

Christ he will be able to follow, and in identifying himself with the Love of God, serve with his whole heart.

Lastly we come to the most neglected form of Prayer: silence. The Quakers feel that even more important than this individual meeting is group silence.[2] Later in this book we can discuss that—just at present we are concerned with the personal religious life.

It is possible to lead our children to value and to know an inner stillness, and to know something of the substance of things not seen. This has been called the experience of solitariness. Our duty is to train children to live in a community, but also to give them the ability to be alone—not to escape, but to be able to face life and grow in solitude when they wish.

You can begin very early—as young as three years old— with some children. "Let's stay still for a minute and think about God." "Let's think how beautiful the trees are this fall." This is prayer-time, too, and the children know it. The time can be extended, and indeed it is extraordinary how noisy, mischievous children love to develop this power of silence within them. The deep gifts of the spirit cannot take root in those who do not know aloneness.

And by some mysterious law we also need the give-and-take and laughter and sharing of pleasures which come from mingling with others: this is also a preparation for other religious experiences,

> Lest the minds of men should become
> Dull, humorless and glum,
> And be tempted to take, even themselves
> Too seriously.[2]

[2] F. W. Harvey, "Ducks," *in Poems of Today* (second series), Sidgwick & Jackson.

So when religious maturity is reached, the whole being is integrated into one purpose. Every great religion recognizes egotism as the root of evil, a destructive force. Salvation comes when the individual can offer himself to God in Christ as a whole person. Only then, in losing his life, does he find it. Worship and prayer are a way of life in God, when we accept the amazing gift of His forgiving love, and through which He sustains us forever.

HELP WITH FAMILY WORSHIP

FERRÉ, NILS, *Family Devotions*. An essay on family prayer in pamphlet form. Obtainable from The Upper Room, 1908 Grand Avenue, Nashville 5, Tennessee

McCAULEY, E. AND L., *A Book of Family Worship,* Scribners

YEO, A. W., *Two Minute Bible Readings,* S.C.M. Press

McCAULEY, L. AND E., *The Book of Prayers,* (A paperback). Dell Publishing Co., 261 Fifth Avenue, New York 16, N.Y.)

MACNUTT, F. B., *The Prayer Manual,* Morehouse

WEISER, F. X., *Handbook of Christian Feasts and Customs,* Harcourt Brace

SEASONAL HELPS

Diocese of Delaware, 2020 Tatnall Street, Wilmington, Delaware

HELPFUL BOOKS ON PRAYER (FOR ADULTS)

COBURN, JOHN B., *Prayer and Personal Religion,* Westminster

WYON, OLIVE, *The School of Prayer,* Allenson

SINCLAIR, RONALD, *When You Pray,* Mowbray

HERMAN, E., *Creative Prayer,* Harper

CHAPTER SIX

Children and Death

Truly, if our faith in Christ were limited to this life only we should, of all mankind, be the most to be pitied!

But the glorious fact is that Christ *did* rise from the dead: He has become the very First to rise of all who sleep the sleep of death. As death entered the world through a man, so has rising from the dead come to us through a Man! As members of a sinful race all men die: as members of the Christ of God shall all men be raised to life, each in his proper order, with Christ the Very First and after Him all who belong to Him when He comes.

(Paraphrase from I Corinthians, Chapter 15, verses 19–23, by J. B. Phillips, in *Letters to Young Churches,* Macmillan)

Death is a part of life. We hope that our children will be able to accept it simply, without the morbid curiosity and the fear so often inflicted from the outside. The child may easily hear the word before we are aware of it, perhaps in casual conversation about animals and plants. Later, when something or somebody dies, he says, "What's dead?"

The child may witness the death of a pet animal, or be confronted with the death of some wild creature in the country. I remember walking in the woods with a three-year-old when we came upon a dead thrush. She regarded it with the greatest astonishment, and informed me that the birdie was asleep. She said we had better go and get him a blanket and some orange juice for when he waked up. She was not asking me about death, and at that particular moment, I did not feel that the perfect time had come for an explanation. Later, other chances presented themselves and were utilized. She readily understood that her body was the house she lived in, that her real self—the thinking, loving part—she could not see. She had put the rather extraordinary question to me, "What could I be that will never die? Could I be a duck?" I do not know why a duck should be especially promising in the way of immortality. Then it was that we talked about the advantage of being a little girl, and she saw that the house of her body was as useless to her without her real self to live in it, as the piano, standing there with no one to play upon it.

Later in a city street, as we were walking together, a flower-covered coffin was carried out of a house as we passed by. She plied me with questions: what was inside the casket? What were they going to do with it? I answered her with the simple facts. "I see," she said, after a thoughtful little pause; "It's a going-away party," and she tripped on ahead in her usual happy way. I think, if the previous conversations had not taken place, she would not have accepted the facts so simply. Immediately after they were told to her, her literal child's mind pursued the question—Why were all those people there? Where were they going? What would they do? Would they come back to the house? It was only after that her own name was evolved, and thereafter a "going-away party" held no terrors for her.

The idea of death always comes as a surprise to a child when it is first confronted. There seems to be something inside us that replies defiantly, "No. Surely this cannot be." If we can handle it wisely, however, we have a wonderful opportunity to help him discern spiritual values. We find ourselves at some unexpected moment asked to explain the vast questions of death and immortality which have been the subject of thought for sages and saints throughout the history of mankind. But its very magnitude should make us beware of complicating the subject, or of trying to tell too much to a tiny child. A queer sound is apt to come into the adult voice. "Why," asks a ruthless observer of our acquaintance, "Why do you sound funny when you say that?" What we need to do is to give them a glimpse of values to which they can hold always.

Death as a *change* which takes place, just as those taking place in the world of Nature, is a parable often used.

Because our whole philosophy of life and religion is challenged when these questions come, and because we want to hold to our original policy of honesty, the examination of our own beliefs is necessary. Did we come by them through real spiritual experience, or have they been superimposed? Some believe in life after death because they have been taught to, and have clung to the conviction almost as to a habit. Others reason it out. Some go by feelings only. Those who have faced death with much-beloved friends frequently have an unreasoning conviction of life-hereafter.

To the Hindu, the soul is essentially immortal, it has always existed, even before birth into this world, and it will exist forever. The Buddhists hope to achieve Nirvana, to become nothingness. The Greek civilization, and others, have held out a hope for the hereafter, but the heaven depicted is often to us far from attractive. The Christian emphasis has always been on the *attainment* of immortal life, on the *quality* of the life here as part of the life hereafter, and described as eternal life. In St. Matthew 25, where the parables of the virgins, the talents, and the judgment are told, we see how Jesus emphasized the importance of the kind of life lived here. It is surely not right to have our children taught that we become flawless as soon as we die, illogical to have them grow up with the notion that we step out of this world into perfection. Is it not more in keeping with the slow growth of the spirit here to assume that, under different and perhaps unobstructed conditions, the life of the spirit continues on its journey, that there is work and opportunity for it to grow, not too suddenly unlike the conditions for its development here?

I know we are touching upon delicate and much-debated points of theology, but parents want some straight arguments. Children who are old enough to be interested in other religions will want that approach. From the Christian viewpoint I can do no better than to quote from the teaching of one of the most vital Christians I know; he gives his own reasons for his belief in eternal life:

"1. First, because it satisfies my mind. If the whole purpose of creation is to produce personality as the highest form of life, then it doesn't make sense that when the goal has been achieved no permanent provision should be made for it—that it could be snuffed out as easily as a candle— that it should be at the mercy of a microbe or be destroyed by the stupidity or sinfulness of man.

"2. Second, because my sense of justice demands it. Even our finite minds can see how terribly unfair it is that some people are given every opportunity while others never have half a chance in this world. Can it be possible that the

Almighty, whose wisdom is infinite, doesn't sense this situation and has no plan to remedy it?

"3. Third, because the very best part of our nature—our unselfish love for other people—cries out that they be given a fair chance to complete their lives. We know that God has made provision for all our other instincts—that He satisfies every legitimate longing of our hearts. Why should we suppose that He will fail us at the point where we need Him most?

"4. Finally, because I believe in Christ. He pledged His word and His life that our faith in the future is justified. He couldn't have spoken with such assurance unless he were absolutely certain of what he was saying. We know that all the rest of His teaching is true. Why, in Heaven's name, should we doubt him at this point? David Livingstone, the great missionary to Africa, when everything seemed hopeless and black before him, wrote in his diary: 'I rely upon the word of a gentleman of the strictest honor.' Here is that word: (the most wonderful and comforting word ever spoken) 'Let not your heart be troubled. Ye believe in God. Believe also in me. In my Father's House are many mansions. If it were not so I would have told you. I go to prepare a place for you. And if I go to prepare a place for you, I will come again and receive you unto myself, that where I am there ye may be also.' " [1]

It is one thing to state your belief in the life everlasting, and another to try to describe the kind of life it will be. We cannot at present know much about that, and we must humbly admit it. We must be careful about the ideas of Heaven a child may absorb. When he looks at ancient pic-

[1] From a sermon by the Rev. Cornelius P. Trowbridge, now Chaplain of St. Luke's Hospital, New York.

79

tures you can tell him that that was the way artists in olden days believed Heaven to be, but we really do not know what it will be like. What modern child wants to wear a long white nightgown and play on a golden harp all day? Their very ideas of God can be affected by the notion that He wants this kind of adoration.

Some children, especially boys, are apparently insensitive to anything but the physical aspects of death, as in animals. They seem callous. An extreme case was cited by an officer who went into a Nazi concentration camp and found he could not resist his instinct to put a boy across his knee and spank him soundly because he found him entirely lacking in the normal human reaction to, and behavior towards, the dead. War erases even the obvious decencies with its crudity. Picture magazines depicting mutilated corpses in great detail, and bad movies, generate insensitiveness and an awareness of only the physical aspect of death.

Mysterious references to undertakers—who now call themselves morticians in order to increase their importance—help to build up morbid curiosity in the mind of the child. Let us answer his questions about the disposal of the human body with simple straightforwardness, dwelling only as much as is necessary on the putting away of "the house we lived in," and concentrating on the more important question of the fulfilling of the work and personality begun here and continued in the hereafter. My experience has been that children can see this more clearly than we do.

I have found it helpful to take a questioning older child to a funeral service I knew would be beautiful, and at which one could be pretty certain that no uncontrolled show of grief would occur. We take our children to baptisms and weddings. If we keep them away from funerals we are relegating those services into the realm of mysteries. The Christian life has the blessing of its fellow-Christians, that worshipping body called the Church—from the cradle to the grave, and beyond.

One particular occasion I have in mind was the funeral service of an old lady for whom the children had a great affection. It was not an untimely death, it had been the quick passing of a full Christian life at a great age. The children had been curious about funerals, and as this was to be in their own familiar church, they went to it. The music, the flowers, the beauty of a purple pall belonging to rich and poor alike were symbols they could understand, and they were a happy revelation. They were impressed by the simple liturgy, especially with the opening, which they spoke of afterwards: "I am the resurrection, and the life: he that believeth in me, though he were dead, yet shall he live: and whosoever liveth and believeth in me shall never die." (St. John 11:25, 26.) We fumble and stumble in our poor human way to try to convey these things, forgetting that we have the whole authority and poetry of Christianity to help us. Conversely, I can see how ideas of death could be cheapened and commercialized by the material show of another type of funeral service.

Easter in all its significance (see Chap. 3), can also do much to strengthen the spiritual conception of death. Men could not kill Christ the Lord. Easter is the season of hope, and victory, and love triumphant, and the realization that the risen Christ can live in us *always*. And again comes the opportunity to re-emphasize the necessity for active loving and serving, the rediscovery of the truth spoken of by St. John—"we know that we have passed from death to life because we love the brethren."

Some of this may seem fairly obvious, but all over the world children are being frightened and hurt through the ignorance of those around them. It is not an uncommon thing, after giving a talk, to have a person come up and ask if something cannot be done about some unfortunate child who is convinced that his mother has been "put in the ground." A foolish nurse, trying to placate a child, told him that if he kissed his dead mother's photograph three times every night, she would come back to him. Others tell a child that their dead father has merely "gone away," and silence him into a terrible bewilderment from which he can be released only by a patient conviction of the truth.

Sometimes there comes to us the opportunity to help bereaved children. To them, dark days show no sign of ending, for to be an unhappy child is to be *completely* unhappy, with no light anywhere in sight, and the feeling that the sorrow will go on forever. They do not measure by past experiences, as an adult would do. If it is only grief at the death of a pet, we shall almost certainly be asked whether animals go to heaven. We can but reply that we see no reason why not: we have no evidence to the contrary.

I am thinking of the irreparable loss of a parent or close friend. How can we possibly help then?

There is of course no one way. Much depends on what ideas the child has about death, and how well we know him. The thing we must spare him at the death of a parent is a period of petting and present-giving from well-meaning grown-ups, which is an artificial form of drugging him, and will leave him lonely when the impulsive wave of sentimentality has died down. He is also in danger of being emotionally "possessed" by the remaining parent or doting aunts, so that his position in the human community and his normal human relationships are out of perspective.

Try to draw him back into the circle as a person of *value,* who has something to bring to it. We have no right to shut him away from experiences which can be an initiation into the deep mysteries of human life, by excluding him from the holiness and tenderness of mutual grief when a loved person dies. We shall try to protect him from hysterical displays of sorrow, but if by being allowed to stay in the family circle the older child finds there is something he can *do* to alleviate the grief of others, you have given him a supreme experience.

The child finds himself loved and wanted through his ability to contribute, and this immediately places his thoughts outside himself and his own loss. It is grown-ups, by their forced cheerfulness which fails to hide the suppressed emotion and pity for the child, who tear his heart to pieces. He either dramatizes himself into a person deserving of much sympathy (a rôle he would not have played had it not been suggested to him), or he feels like a girl I knew when a child, whose idolizing cousins asked her to give the dolls' nativity play she usually entertained them with at Christmas, before her mother died. She said in desperation, "Yes, I'll give it, if you don't all sit there with tears in your eyes." Here the relation with the mother had been deep and loving, and she knew instinctively that they were trespassing into the part of her life in which she must bear her loss alone.

First, then, let the child be an integral part of the human community. Then let other wise adults try to replace the parent to some extent. Perhaps they can at least hold up the ideals which bound him to the lost one, being to him what we have described before as "religion in activity," letting him know that there's someone who cares about him very much, while realizing that there are some dark places to which he must go alone, while he makes his individual terms with grief.

And, in case we become too involved in our thinking, let me tell you about Edward. He is now a grown man, and he told me the story himself. I think it may have been part of the immovable structure of his present Christian life. When Edward was about eight years old he had a great friend, a man called John who was an employee of his father, in their country home. He taught Edward to fish, and they spent whole days together, walking and talking in the closest understanding that can come through sharing country ways. Then, quite suddenly, John died.

Edward's nurse tried to break the news to him. She stumbled over her words and was so embarrassed that she gave it up. Then his mother tried to break the news to him, again unsuccessfully. Edward came to the rescue.

"Are you trying to tell me," he asked, "that the part of John I could see has died, and the rest of him has gone to heaven?"

He says he does not know where his convictions came from, but he thinks they may have been conveyed by John himself, who was not cumbered with too many theories about the universe.

The way we can help our own children, or those well-known to us, is usually clearer to us than the way to help strangers, for we know what has gone before. Sooner or later in everyone's life comes the opportunity to help or hinder a child bearing a burden of loss or suffering. It will depend on *the child's idea of God*. Perhaps his very faith in God as a loving Father may be destroyed.

An eleven-year-old wrote down, quite spontaneously, her thoughts about God to one of her parents, when she was away from home:

"These are some times when I feel God near: One day last spring when you told me I had to go to Camp, I leaned out of the window of the subway and I felt I was near God. Another time I was very homesick and I lay with my face in the pillow. Then I felt that God was so near I felt I knew what love was. How happy I was, yet sad. And once I was swimming. The sky was blue and I felt God in the clouds. I was so happy. I was thankful. I know what thanks is. I know God."

Nearly every child will say at some time in its life, when confronted by loss or disaster, "I can't understand why God lets it happen." We are confronted, in a moment, with the great problem of suffering. Just as in facing the mystery of death, we can but offer our own ideas in this, with the same humility which can leave the child to go further than we may be able to do. Most children can grasp, if they are old enough to ask the question, that if we did not have free will we should be but puppets in the universe. They can also see that just as our love for each other is part of God's love for us, so there is no suffering in the world which is not ultimately endured by God. Tremendous thoughts, but through the knowledge of God as a loving Father, and the life and teachings of Jesus, it is possible to sow their seed in some measure. When others are torn away from us, God does not let us go.

The Christian understanding of death is founded upon the Resurrection and Ascension of Jesus Christ. We believe in "the forgiveness of sins, the Resurrection of the Body, and the Life Everlasting," for "by means of death He hath overcome death." We have in Christ a *new* relationship with God, and through Him we have the unearned gift of eternal life.

We shall not be disembodied spirits, for man is a soul-body, a being in totality. We do not know how we shall receive our second bodies any more than we understand fully exactly how we received the ones we have now. There is a close similarity between our birth into this world and our re-birth into the world to come.

Parents who are themselves confused will confuse their children, and it is essential that we should think our way through to the Christian view of death. In Dr. Casserley's book, *No Faith of My Own* (see the list on page 216) he gives on pages 92–94 statements which will be very helpful, and so does Bishop Pike on pp. 111 and following of *Beyond Anxiety*.

The most important fact for us to know and believe is that we cannot be separated from God unless we deliberately wish it, and continually run away from His Loving Presence. The heart of what we must teach our children lies in St. Paul's great affirmation (Romans 8:38, 39).

> "Neither death, nor life, nor angels, nor principalities, nor powers, nor things present, nor things to come, nor height, nor depth, nor any other creature, shall be able to separate us from the love of God, which is in Christ Jesus our Lord."

CHAPTER SEVEN

Should Church Schools Exist?

"O God Who has sent Thy beloved Son to be the Way, the Truth and the Life, grant that we, looking unto Him, may set forward the teaching power of Thy Church, to the nurture of Thy children, the increase of Thy Kingdom, and the glory of Thy Son, Jesus Christ our Lord." Amen

What is the purpose of the church school, or Sunday school, in these times, and why does it continue to exist? Is it more likely to spoil a child's attitude towards religion, so that he discards any interest in it as soon as his intellect is sufficiently developed to criticize the teaching he receives; will he become smug, and filled with a spurious, lukewarm goodness; or will it help him to develop a deep and indestructible religious life, rooted in intellect and feeling, and tradition strengthened by vision?

I believe it depends chiefly on the reality and depth of the religious life of those who teach him, their education, training, and above all, their religious experience; in other words, what they ARE, and secondly, what and how they teach.

We must not make sweeping statements; it is not right to

judge all church schools together, for as in day schools, there are good, bad, and indifferent. Even within them, some classes may be excellent, others poor. The best ministers and directors cannot, with a wave of the wand, produce a set of eminently well-equipped teachers for kindergarten upwards.

Perhaps, at some far-distant time, church schools will no longer be needed. That will be when every family—or most families—are capable of offering a well-rounded religious education to the child, when the leaders in day school education have re-thought the whole educational process, when the spirit of materialism and lack of respect for personality is not uppermost. Even if this happy condition eventually comes, is there still nothing left for the church school to offer?

I think we are agreed that the church school is a supplement to home life, not a substitute for it, and also it might be possible for us to discover that it has something not available in home or day school. We may consider, also, whether the family pew is an alternative, and what of the districts where good teachers are not forthcoming?

The need of the world today is to learn to perceive some reality beyond that which is seen. Our children belong both to the contemporary world and to the future. If they cannot find a way of solving the problems that confront them, this civilization will perish. All this has been said before. If humanity today is blind to everything but the things of the sense, and is perhaps groping after a vague general truth, surely the only way to turn the tide is for those who have seen the light, however dimly, to point out to others a way of finding it for themselves. We must obey God or perish.

If we have faith only in historic fulfillment we deceive ourselves: too long have we looked back and compared past experiences. Man has unknown powers, which we call faith, which will not come to fruition until he learns to trust them instead of one social scheme after another, which he continues to substitute for the real relationship with his God, called religion. He tries to create his own destiny, without allying himself to the Creator of the universe; fear and cold reason shut him off from the Source. Can we make the church schools a place where faith can be nurtured, and if not, who will save this generation from paganism?

We all know the position in our public schools today: it exists also in many of the private ones. Because our schools are attended by Protestants, Catholics, and Jews, the State argues that it is constitutionally impossible to teach religion, and takes the illogical line of pretending that religion does not exist. The result of this is that the non-believers cannot be called agnostics, or even atheists, for to belong to one of these groups suggests that you have grounds for disagreement, they have caught the policy of the State; they are unaware that religious problems exist, and live in a spiritual vacuum, which too often means ethical vacuum also. The growing number of parochial schools outside the Roman communion give evidence to the concern of parents.

Those who are anxious to have teaching *about* religion in the schools (not to be confused with trying to indoctrinate the children with sectarian beliefs), argue that every other great influence and trend of today is presented in the schools—economics, history, literature, art and music—but religion as a part of our culture is ignored, although fifty per cent of the population go to church. The King James version of the Bible is not even taught in the English course, despite the fact that it is the greatest piece of literature in the English tongue. Would it be possible to study the greatest parts of the Bible in adolescence without being affected by them, if only ethically?

In some states the system of "released time" (unfortunate title), or "dismissed time," has been tried, or is being tried. Children, whose parents are willing, go to some suitable building near the school in order to receive religious instruction. Attendance is recorded and in some cases teachers approved by the public school authorities are employed, which at least indicates some form of supervision. Children who do not attend are given either some ethical, non-religious instruction, or a study period.

This plan has been surveyed in various districts, and it is reported that in a few of them it is going well; where the scheme has earned itself a good status in the community, it is proving very useful. At least it gives more time and therefore more opportunity for religious teaching. Most important of all, it is an attempt to bring religious teaching into relation with school life and everyday life, and should make it much easier to correlate studies in ways previously mentioned, to tie up with the child's geography, history and other studies. Working effectively it should tend to raise the quality of religious teaching, but the hopes originally entertained, that it would reach the fifty per cent "unchurched," have not materialized up to now.

Among the arguments against this plan of "released time," is the contention that in many places the churches have proved themselves not yet ready for it; above all, they have not enough trained people who are qualified in this field to teach well, and since two minuses will not make a plus, one more period of indifferent religious teaching will not fulfill the purpose for which it was designed. Often there is a lack of sufficient money and equipment. In some places the very words "released time" have come to imply a time when discipline is at a low ebb, and the authorities lending public buildings for the purpose have sad tales to tell of damage done to property. But it does look as though the scheme can be effective where the right people are available to see it through: we always come back to the question of *individuals*.

One way some parents solve the question of giving what they feel to be the right beginnings in religious education, is insistence on attendance at church in the family pew. Many will tell you with firm pride that they have taken their children to church with them every Sunday since they were two or three years old.

Champions of the family pew say that the children "get something" from the music, and fellowship, and the atmosphere of the church. Of course they do. The children themselves maintain that they like to go and sit with their parents. The parents say you cannot start a good habit too early, and certainly many of our Sunday schools offer a poor substitute for these blessings. Perhaps the solution lies in attendance at part of the family service, with classes during the sermon. Every church has its own problems of preference, locality and transportation.

Those who are opposed to this custom base their arguments on two facts, the children are bored and worry the older people with their fidgeting, they contend; and the children are conditioned into thinking that religion is a lot of meaningless words, because they "don't understand."

Taking these contentions one at a time, I would say in reply to the first that many parishes *are not ready* to have the children at the big services. The older people cast such reproving looks at young mothers whose babies give a few cheerful chirps that the mothers are unable to worship or to listen. Now when babies scream loudly and long they should obviously be removed for the sake of everyone, but I am speaking of the happy noises they make which are really their method of joining the congregation. One would have thought that if the Church is the Family of God these sounds could be either ignored or appreciated, according to the disposition of the older generation. But older people who do not know that these infants are part of "the whole congregation of Christ's flock" need to be helped, it is a question of change of attitude. Many churches have nurseries for the very young, with cots provided. If these are really well-run and the babies happy, it is an excellent way of freeing the parents and placating the older members who object to their presence.

As to the second contention, that the children do not understand, we can only answer "No, of course they do not." Much religious education goes on on the unconscious levels. There is nothing we can offer a child as a substitute for the experience of sitting with his parents and of knowing himself to be a part of the Family of God. The very fact of seeing adults worship and of knowing that these adults he believes to be so powerful look up to God the Father as a Person to be worshipped, is something it is impossible to teach in words.

Most parents, in services where there are long sermons and where no provision is made for the children elsewhere, take a simple toy with them—I am sure this has been done for many generations.

As this book is read by people of many denominations, it is impossible to meet the needs of all of them, as services differ so much. To Episcopalians I would say that where there is a Parish Communion, if they have helped their children as they grow to see some of the great moments in the liturgical action, they have undoubtedly found that the children from a very early age are quite enthralled by what is going on. If parents insist on sitting in a part of the church where the children can see nothing but pillars, or the backs of adults, or even the top of the pew, they are certainly going to be naughty, and they will receive nothing by "osmosis."

In these brief remarks I do not mean to imply that what is seen is all that counts, and I would suggest that those who want to think about this problem a little more should read what I have said on the subject in my book *The Privilege of Teaching* (Morehouse).

Let us also face the difficulties encountered by those trying to build a good church school. The most formidable, and sometimes unsurmountable, is that of finding good teachers. Trained people who teach all the week are generally too tired to begin again when Sunday comes; or they feel they want the regenerating experience of going to church themselves. A few, seeing the need, come in and help magnificently; others are willing to help, but although they have all the techniques of teaching, they have no religious convictions and withdraw on grounds of agnosticism.

To be *willing* to teach, to be *ready* to help, is not enough. The butt of journalist and playwright is "Dear Miss So-and-So, who has taught Sunday school for thirty years." Some people, with real inspiration and natural insight, *have* taught in Sunday school, and kindled a religious spark which continues to grow in many a good life, but how many more have offered the sugar-coated sentimentality we have spoken of before, and have not been able to maintain the interest, let alone the respect, of the enquiring mind? No wonder parents, looking backwards, have been afraid to send their children to Sunday school. They argue that religion is a delicate and indescribable experience which will be ruined by such mistreatment. True. But if we can find for our children people in whom we can trust, is it not probable that an effective program of Christian Education, which will include the three elements of Worship, Study, and Service, may prove to be the very thing for which we are seeking, which will help to provide the foundation of rock for a young religious life? While acknowledging that we cannot teach religion as we would mathematics, we must keep before us the necessity for such a foundation, and the need for trained teachers to build it.

The more I consider the question of church schools, the more clear it becomes that, in the limited time at the disposal of the leaders, one invaluable thing they can help to create is the right *attitude* of the child towards religion. It is in our hands—the child will either assume that the search for God is a great pursuit in which he wishes to join, or we can bore him, or make him unhappy, so that the very word religion is degraded.

Some of the finest church school teachers are found in the parents themselves, who, under church leadership, bring their enthusiasm to the work, and are determined to build the school the children should have. The privilege of working with these people, and watching their convictions grow as they move along with the children (so many of whom give us much more than we can offer them), is a great joy. Coming from the same environment as the children they teach, they can enter into their lives in a way no "imported" teacher can do, and the relationship has nothing of artificiality about it.

We should rid ourselves of the notion that religious education is largely to be undertaken by women. Men are needed just as much. At a certain age it is imperative that a boy should have a man to interpret religion to him, to face his problems "as man to man," and to represent those peculiarly masculine interests in his life and hopes, showing him that all his work and all his play belong to the pattern of Christian living, and can be offered to God.

Many men with a deepened conviction of the necessity for religion in our world have arrived at that conviction through severe experience, and have a contribution to offer the new generation which cannot be overestimated. If they will come into the fight against evil, their time and effort will bring a rich harvest. Fortunately a number of these men have decided to go into the ministry, and those under whom they train testify to the incalculable value of what they bring to their vocation.

To give a practical illustration of the kind of work possible, I have in mind a class of ten seventh-grade boys, that is, aged about twelve years old, who in the fifth grade had a reputation for organized wickedness in Sunday school and despised it utterly. The following year, a parent of the kind I have described as making a good teacher had the courage to take them on. He had, besides a really active religious life, a fine mind and a sense of humor. He became extremely fond of the boys, and they of him. They had their bad times, but there grew up in them a respect for Christianity and the church. Several of them became officials on the Junior Church Council, and helped in practical ways when they were needed —with the Christmas play, ushering at special services, helping with Thanksgiving baskets for an orphanage, and so on. In the spring after the end of the war, they saw a United Nations film at one of the assemblies during a church school session, and not long after decided that they wanted to give a Peace Service in the church. The minister was interested, and let them take over the first part of the morning service attended by the whole congregation. The rest of the older children worked on a choric prayer, and the Junior Choir sang the anthem. The heading printed at the top of the order of service was provided spontaneously by one of the boys, partly his own composition, partly remembered from what he had heard or read—he called it "A Prayer." The Junior Sermon was the result of many weeks thinking and discussion by the seventh grade boys which they finally summarized with their teacher's help. It was delivered from the lectern by one of the boys. After the young people went down to their classes during the third hymn, the minister preached on the same theme, taking for his text, "There is a lad here . . ." and discussing the importance of Christianity in the new generation. The ushers were boys from the sixth grade, and the whole contribution of the normally lively modern children was one of dignity and responsibility. The officials of the church later wrote them a formal letter of thanks. Those who were present were deeply moved by the simple honesty of the young people's worship, and the church family felt itself to be united in a universal cause. Most important was the experience for the children, they were giving themselves to the cause they believed in.

The following is the order of service used, and the sermon written by the boys:

A PRAYER

O God of Peace, help us to obey Thy laws. Thou callest us to feed the hungry, to clothe the naked, to defend man's rights and God's rights, to win back men's hearts to Thee by man's trust in Thee.

(Adapted by Lincoln Hansel)

FOURTH SUNDAY IN LENT
10:30 A.M. MORNING PRAYER AND SERMON

Organ Prelude: "Oh Hail this day" . . . J. S. Bach
Processional, Hymn ("Lead on, O King Eternal").
Choric Prayer: . . . St. Francis of Assisi

Lord, make me a channel of Thy peace—
    That where there is hatred I may bring love,
    That where there is wrong I may bring the spirit of
      forgiveness,
    That where there is discord I may bring harmony,
    That where there is error I may bring truth,
    That where there is doubt I may bring faith,
    That where there is despair I may bring hope,
    That where there are shadows I may bring Thy light,
    That where there is sadness I may bring joy.
Lord, grant that I may seek rather to comfort than to be
    comforted,
    To understand rather than to be understood,
    To love than to be loved,
    For it is by giving that one receives,
    It is by self-forgetting that one finds,
    It is by forgiving that one is forgiven,
    It is by dying that one awakens to eternal life.

THE LESSON (Micah 4:1–5)
Junior Sermon (see below)
Anthem: "My Soul, there is a country"   J. S. Bach

      My soul, there is a country
      Afar beyond the stars,
      Where stands a wingèd sentry
      All skilful in the wars.
      There, above noise and danger,
      Sweet Peace sits crowned with smiles,

97

And One born in a manger
Commands the beauteous files.

Henry Vaughan

Hymn ("I sing a song of the saints of God")
Children then left the church, Adult service continued.

The *Junior Sermon,* delivered by a member of the class who wrote it, was:

WHAT CAN WE DO FOR WORLD PEACE?

"In the fourteenth verse of the second chapter of the gospel according to St. Luke are these words we all know: "On earth peace, good will toward men." Peace, good will toward men!

"What can we do for peace?

"Should we kill all our enemies? It looks easy. Somebody may think we could just take a few atom bombs and blow them up. Maybe we could; but if we did, we would always be afraid somebody would do it to us. If we tried to bomb each enemy, we would surely have an enemy left somewhere, and would make more and more enemies by such conduct. Sooner or later one of them would bomb us, and finally there would be nobody left. The thing to do is to make the United Nations so strong that no one will dare to start another war.

"Should we try to take care of everybody? We can't. We can't feed and clothe the whole world. If we tried, we would all become poor without giving others enough to eat and to wear, and we might be blamed instead of thanked. Other countries would rather become independent than weak and dependent upon us.

"What we must do is to help other people help themselves. We must treat different races the same way. We

98

must give everyone a fair chance and a fair start. We must give them not only food, but seed.

"Most important of all, we must understand other people. We can't just hand them something and forget them. We should make them feel that we like them and are interested in them and want them to stand on their own feet and live with us as their friends.

"All this we can do best as Christians. We must again take Christianity into heathen countries. We should teach, but not force. And the things we should teach are the things taught by Christ.

"We can begin by being good Christians ourselves; so that just as Christianity has spread to families, to cities and to countries, it can be spread by Christians to the whole world."

The following year, as seventh graders, they wrote and delivered another sermon:

"In the ninth verse of the thirteenth Chapter of the Gospel according to St. Matthew, Jesus said: "Who hath ears to hear, let him hear."

"If a newspaper reporter should stop you on your way out of Church today and ask you what you got out of the service, and you told the truth, what would you say?

"Would you have to admit that you had come here to pass the time—if the weather was bad—or just to talk to the neighbors? If you were asked what the lessons were about, would you know? And did you pray, or while the minister was saying prayers for you, did your thoughts wander?

"Suppose the reporter asked about your children. Would you have to plead guilty to bribing your children to come to Church, to frightening them by saying they'd not get into Heaven unless they come to Church, or to forcing them to go without any idea of what Church is for? It is hard to make a child believe in God if his parent does not. It is hard for a boy or girl to know what is expected of him in Church if he is not told something beforehand at home. He will realize he comes here not to fool, but to worship—if you do. And he can understand what God is like if you say only that you come to Church to confess your sins and that if you do God will help you—that He isn't angry, but you should not sin any more.

"God is the Reporter, asking you that question today. He is here, in and outside of Church, on Sunday and all the rest of the week, asking you not what you got out of Church, but what you put in."

Before going on further to discuss what is offered in Sunday school, we should consider those districts where, after the most diligent searching, the trained leaders find that they are unable to provide the right teachers to carry out a good program of Christian education. They decide that the available standard of teaching is far below that of the day schools, that the children are bored, and the morale bad. They come to the conclusion that they will try to provide classes up to a certain stage—sometimes through fourth grade, sometimes to a lower grade—and they run the kind of junior church which is not an addition to the regular classes for those of nine or ten years old and upwards, but a system of religious education to include worship and instruction at the same time, where all the children meet together in the church, usually before the adult service. Their own officers take part in the ushering, take up the collection, sing in the choir. The service is of course shaped to their age and needs. It is rather like the adult one in plan, and certainly keeps the formality and dignity, which our children enjoy today—they have so little of it anywhere else. There is a Bible lesson of instruction before the Bible reading, and the minister or trained leader sees to it that the services are part of a careful plan.

The success of this method depends on the ability of the leader to talk to children—he must be a good teacher, and what he offers must be of lasting value. The stories, if there are stories, should not be a weekly entertainment, devised simply to catch their attention. It can at its best be a way of *growing* into the church family, instead of being a mere onlooker. It is not a substitute for worshipping with the whole congregation.

There can be no true unification of self, or "conversion" the surrender of the self to a Higher Will—if the individual remains solitary. Nor is it enough, obviously, if his relations are only with that of his immediate family, and then the immediate community. As he grows, we want the Christian to extend his interests to include the whole world, with all mankind as his brothers. As we have seen, even though he may come from a religious home, he gets no teaching about religion from his day school, whereas the aim of the effective church school is to help the child, from his earliest years, to participate in those experiences which can lead toward the *full* realization of his life. It provides, as part of the necessities for fulfillment, *corporate* worship, study, service, and, where necessary, during the week recreation. Instead of feeling itself to be a curiosity in a pagan world, the child also has the happiness of Christian friendships, just as he does at youth conferences which can later reinforce his strength, and where his questions are answered.

If our desire in religious training is to help the child to discover the Will of God in his life, and since it is true that the Will of God at the human level seems to demonstrate itself through the give and take of human relationships, are we not depriving the child very seriously if we do not let him share in the Christian relationships available to him in the good Sunday school? I think our conduct is justified if we keep our children out of a school where we feel his religious standards are lowered, where there is no creative experience and the teaching is poor.

There should be, in every plan for the religious education of the child, opportunities to discover what led *others* to God, and also, in the present day, comparison of different religions. At one Protestant church school, a Rabbi came to address one of their assemblies, and the next Sunday, a sixth grade teacher tried to answer the enquiries of his class on these lines:

"Last Sunday Rabbi Cohen came to talk to us about the Jewish Religion. You know there are a good many people who don't like the Jews; in fact there are too many people who have the idea that anyone with beliefs about God different from their own are wicked and must be inferior. This is called intolerance and prejudice, and we don't think it is a good way to think about other people. It is sometimes hard not to feel this way, but really it is rather stupid of us. You see the truth is we can't any of us really understand all about God because He is too big and wonderful for us to understand: we can only try and understand Him partly.

"Suppose I try and explain what I mean by a 'parable' —that is by a story which gives you the idea. Have you ever tried looking straight at the sun on a bright day? If you have, you know that your eyes aren't strong enough to see it clearly—it's too bright and it blinds you, and so you can't see its outline clearly. But if you look at it through a piece of colored glass you can see it quite well. Some people can see it best through smoked glass, and others see better by using red glass, or green, or blue—whatever color suits their own eyes best. If a lot of people look at the sun through different colored glass it will look different to each of them: some will see it red and some green, and so on, and one will say it is red and another will say it is green. But really of course it isn't either, for all these people see through their pieces of glass is part of the light coming from the sun, for they aren't able to see it all and the shape as well. But what each sees comes from the same sun, only each sees only part of that light. Well, let us call God like the sun, and the different religions are the pieces of colored glass—the Protestants and the Roman Catholics and the Jews, and a number of others too. We all see the same God but we each see Him through our particular piece of colored glass, and one color enables some people to see best and another helps others to see most clearly, according to the kind of spiritual eyes he has. If you can see best through a red glass you may say to the next person 'God is red,' and the other one will say to you 'No, He is green,' and then you might get into a great argument about it and each think the other is wrong. But if you really understand the matter better you would rather say, 'We both see Him round and very bright: I can see Him best through my piece of red glass, but of course we are both looking at the same God, and if you can see Him better through a green glass go ahead, so long as you can see best that way.'

"Now Jesus could see God more clearly than any of us can—He had better eyes. He invented a kind of glass specially adapted for the clear seeing of God and he taught people to use it. But still there were lots of people whose eyes were not good enough to use Jesus' new glass, and they thought they could see better with the old glass that they had been using before—the glass we call the Jewish Religion. Just remember that they too are looking at God through the glass which they think shows Him most clearly to them."

The helpful discussions which followed, would, I think have been unlikely to occur under different conditions, for here were ten eager people looking for the truth, and here was a sympathetic man to guide them.

What, then, can the church school offer in the way of study? It will vary in different districts. The standards of day school attainment are not the same everywhere. Wherever possible the day school curriculum should be known to those planning the Sunday classes. As close a cooperation as possible should be maintained in every way. The supervisors of most schools are sympathetic when they see capable people out to help their pupils. And in matters of conduct and character they can give invaluable observations, because they see the children over a longer period of time. The idea of coordination has been suggested previously, as in the instance of teaching about Joseph and Moses during the year they are studying Egypt in school.

In certain private schools, especially in boarding schools, important work is being done which may well inspire new courses in Sunday schools. One, for example, has taken for its theme (for older boys) the tragic predicament of human life, beginning with the study of King Lear, then turning to the gospel tragedy, and finally the possibilities of contemporary Christianity. Another school took the history of various religious leaders who opposed the Nazi rule—one could use other figures in history—and then passed on to the life of Christ, *beginning* with the Crucifixion, then studying the events which led up to it, including Jesus' earlier ministry, and going on to the Resurrection and the early church.

A third scheme, worked out at a Sunday school which was being reorganized in a Parish where previous training had been almost nil, was to give the children from ten years old up a picture of the search for God, painted, as it were, with a big brush. From September to Easter they studied highlights of the Old Testament, showing how the patriarchs as prophets sought for an unknown God who revealed Himself to them as the centuries passed, and how He revealed Himself in His Son. Christmas from that angle meant something deeper to them when it came. From then until Easter they considered certain events in the life of Christ, with Easter as another climax. After Easter came the Early Christians and the beginning of the church. The idea was to give them a very broad conception of the foundations of our faith, and how it might fit into the plan for the world today. Then the following year they were able to develop sections of the plan in detail, having got in touch with the children and roused their interests. With several classes doing the same thing, it was possible to show movies, and to get folios of pictures from the Museum of Fine Arts, to illustrate some of the work.

This book is not a treatise on curricula, and detailed programs of Christian education are available in many other places, but it might be helpful to survey what is often taught successfully. Following the natural growth of the children's minds, the good church school usually offers, for the tiny children up to five years old, experiences of sharing and being happy within the Church family. Some people have described these as "godward experiences." They like to visit the church, both when it is empty, for a little pilgrimage, and for short periods during the services. They come of course to participate in the big festivals—Christmas, Easter, Thanksgiving—for which they are carefully prepared. They, and first grade, have simple Bible stories, especially about Jesus, with good pictures and little hymns and songs. The closer the cooperation of parents and teachers, the more effective the work will be. Parents are usually at liberty to visit when they wish, and should be told of the plans for the work as it goes on.

In grade two, at least for part of the year, it is usual to give some idea of Palestinian life, a background for much of their study. They will stage their Bible stories in this day and age until they have to re-learn the setting as it was. I do not think this is a serious thing, but it is easier to understand the stories Jesus told, and His parables, as well as the events of His life as revealed in the gospels, if we know something of His surroundings. Until then, when children draw their Bible stories for you, they will always be in modern guise. I have been presented with the story of Hagar and Ishmael (at a time when I had no choice in the stories told), in which Ishmael is being pushed briskly across the desert in a modern American baby carriage. Another little boy drew the Wise Men in the Nativity scene arriving in Ford cars. I also like to remember the little colored boy who painted the manger scene. "Why," said the other children crowding round him, "you've made the baby colored!" "He is colored to me," said the little boy. Surely this shows the universal appeal of the Christ.

Grade two will also continue to study the life of Jesus until they can begin to look at it, in a simple way, as a whole. All children love narrative, and a good teacher has to know how to tell a story. The children respond eagerly, if you make the Bible "come alive" to them. Their perception amazes us. I have in mind a day when I told the story of Zacchaeus (St. Luke 19). They felt all the suspense of those crowds waiting to see Jesus of Nazareth, and all the drama of the moment when He said, pointing up to the tree, "Zacchaeus, make haste and come down; for today I must abide at thy house." We had talked of the probable unpopularity of Zacchaeus, and when I asked, "Do you think it was a good idea for the people to avoid him?" many of the seven-year-old listeners called out, "Yes, serve him right," but one thoughtful boy remarked, "I don't, it would make him worse than ever, make him more shy." And then again, after Zacchaeus had come down from the sycamore tree and "received Him joyfully into his house," I asked, "why do you suppose Jesus visited Zacchaeus, why didn't He choose someone else?" "Because He wanted to make him good," announced the class. "No," said the young philosopher, "He chose Zacchaeus because he wanted to show the village how to treat bad people." How many adults could go as far as that?

In schools where grade three "graduates" from the Primary Department into the Junior Department, they will perhaps study such themes as "discovering our church," helping them to prepare for more active participation in church life. They usually receive a Bible to mark this milestone, and it is logical in fourth grade to learn how to find their way around in the Bible, to learn how it came to be, and to discover the stories in it which they have known for such a long time. Some with home training will already be fairly familiar with it. Nearly all children are puzzled as to why its language is different from our own.

From grade five upwards there are endless possibilities, some of which have already been mentioned. Everything can now be studied at a higher level, to fit the maturing needs of the young people. Their Bible study continues, in both Old and New Testaments, always giving much time to the Life of Christ, and the application of its message to the modern world. There is church history, and in some communities, the study of the Prayer Book. Older classes like courses in personal religion: they want to discuss their own problems. The syllabus grows out of the needs of the children, and the questions they ask. An occasional testing will reveal many surprises.

It is helpful to both parents and teachers if an annual report on every pupil is sent to the home. The following extracts from actual reports may be of interest:

REPORT NO. 1

Timothy is a gentleman and a good citizen. He has been elected Vice-President of the Junior Church Council by the other boys and girls in the church school and deserved this tribute and responsibility. In a group which once established a reputation for intentional chaos, he has not only behaved himself but simultaneously kept the respect of more turbulent spirits. There was, of course, one occasion when he went on a frolic of his own; but he was tempted less by insurrectionism than by the greener grass on the other side of the fence. He talks frankly and fairly and has the mental and emotional balance of an older boy.

In the more scholastic aspects of his course this year, Timothy did not at first do as well as he might, or, be it said in all justice to him, as well as he desired. We have hesitated to assign outside work fearing to make unfair demands on boys whose study time was already full; but the result has been that Timothy has felt a lack of guidance. Only recently were we thus able to analyze the reason Timothy was not getting more out of his course. Given a standard and an outline of what was expected of him, his improvement was sensational. He ended the year doing honor work.

Next year in grade seven we shall continue our effort to give Timothy and others more direction without too much additional work.

REPORT NO. 2

Kenneth is in danger of trying to make double plays before he gets hold of the ball. He has an unusual command of fact and language, but he is almost too quick—his mind leaps from one idea to another and on to a third, sometimes without adequate attention to the first. He learns some things so easily that he fails to learn them well. Despite a jittery tendency to do almost anything different from what is going on, the general level of his school work has been of honor grade, and he has been not only conscientious but an imaginative leader in student government and of real service to the church.

REPORT NO. 3

Some boys impertinently, egotistically, and obstreperously challenge their teachers to teach them anything. Peter politely, unconsciously, and quietly challenges his teacher to teach him more than the teacher first thought the lesson contained. Neither as brilliant nor as quick as some, Peter makes more substantial and eventually greater progress because of real understanding, a finely balanced sense of proportion, and a straightforward, cooperative attitude that says: "The situation may be peculiar and none of my business but what can I do to help?" His school work in the early part of the year was steady and he gradually improved it to high honor calibre at the end of the year for what a day school would call a B average. No grade would do justice to his thoughtful originality, sturdy independence, and almost intuitive sense of ethics. He is the kind of a boy every father prays to get for a son.

REPORT NO. 4

Paul has brought his Bible to class more than any other boy and enjoyed reading it.

However, he has come so seldom, and when he did come spent so much time in giggling and in trying to distract the other boys and the teacher, that he has given little attention to the work being done. Even after liberal allowance for the normal restlessness of boys Paul's age, it is obvious from his average grade of 22 out of a possible 100 that he has failed to do or to understand as much as he should in order to obtain promotion.

In these circumstances, therefore, Paul probably would be unable to cope next year with the more difficult work planned for the seventh grade, and he should stay in grade six. The subjects studied in grade six next year will be somewhat different from the course this past year and he may have a different teacher; so that there should be enough novelty in the work to interest him; and he should eventually benefit from the opportunity for more thorough application to study at the grade six level which another year there will give him.

REPORT NO. 5

Tom has the most maturely balanced and sensitive mind in the sixth grade of the church school. He is not as quick as some, nor has he as flashy a memory as others; but he insists on being thorough. When he learns something, he has a complete picture which he retains. He is not satisfied with parroting superficial or second-hand comments; he seeks to and does get at the heart of matters under discussion. He has a direct, sincere, and unself-conscious religious feeling and is willing and able to fight for what he is convinced is right.

Already Tom has a clear idea of the kind of work he wants to do and the kind of man he wants to be. For him there is no line of demarcation between a pious Sunday and a materialistic Monday. We are sure he will lead a life of real service as a vigorous Christian gentleman; and we selfishly hope we may have the pleasure of knowing him not only next year in seventh grade but for many years to come.

REPORT NO. 6

Walter has been most faithful in attendance and has shown great improvement in his attitude toward his work and some improvements in the work itself. Earlier in the year, he handicapped himself by inattention; but thanks to help from his mother he has made a real effort to take part in the work of the class.

Of course it has been Walter himself who had to work out his own problems. They have not been easy for him and he has not wholly solved them. He is growing fast and is therefore so active that he cannot sit still for any length of time. His mind as well as his body is jumpy. This is not anything for which we consider he is to blame but a condition with which we cope as best we can. He finds it hard to express himself in writing. Nevertheless, when he has become interested in what the class was doing he has talked intelligently on matters which he recognized as important. He has, however lively, been energetic rather than disrespectful, and has been direct in thought and frank in speech. Above all, he has from time to time shown real understanding of the situation studied and of the problems and personalities of the great characters in the Bible, sometimes with guidance and other times on his own initiative.

Our children need help in discovering the work of the church of today and its relation to the future. They need time for teaching and discussion of Christian beliefs. When our American delegation of young people went as representatives to the religious conference at Amsterdam, they came back saying they had been cheated, they said they could not discuss doctrine, as the delegates from other countries could do; words like salvation and grace were not in their vocabularies. They came home demanding discussion of faith and doctrine, and they also wanted better Bible teaching. When we see the magnitude of all this, we realize the trained leadership required.

Opportunities for service come with all this study, again depending on the district where the children live. There is no point in making artificial needs, the real chances come, but they should grow out of the children's own knowledge and wishes. Many want to work for the relief of those abroad, some see their opportunity nearer home, even within their own church.

Some Sunday school leaders, working hand in hand with the public schools, have discovered that afternoon clubs for children who come out of school at 2:30 are a great blessing to the community. Many children coming home find parents still out at work—and that is where much trouble begins. Such organizations would seem to me a way of supplying some of the richer influences pitifully lacking in some children's lives, chances for producing plays, and learning crafts, if only some will care enough to begin.

No boy or girl can read the Bible as the self-revelation of God, study it, and the character and life of Jesus as portrayed in the gospels under the right guidance, without being profoundly affected. Dullness has been called the unforgivable sin in Bible teaching: of this we have been criminally guilty. Our time is limited, and the tradition has already been built up for children to leave the church school too early. But for those who will come into the fray, we can offer the experience of contributing something towards "the great unfinished task of the Kingdom of God."

Would not these possibilities indicate, that until we can find elsewhere what the effective church school can offer, these schools should continue to exist? If they do not, or if they are so badly organized as to be useless, who will show our children the way?

Children and Religion

BOOKS TO HELP TEACHERS AND SUPERINTENDENTS

ON ADMINISTRATION

VIETH, PAUL H., *The Church School,* Christian Education Press, Philadelphia

HEIM, RALPH D., *Leading a Sunday Church School,* Muhlenberg Press

A REFERENCE BOOK

(Ed. by Marvin Taylor), *Religious Education:* A Comprehensive Survey, Abingdon

FOR TEACHERS

LOBINGIER, JOHN, *If Teaching Is Your Job,* Pilgrim Press

BERKELEY, JAMES P., *You Can Teach,* Judson Press

HOAG, VICTOR, *It's Fun to Teach,* Morehouse

HIGHET, GILBERT, *The Art of Teaching,* Knopf. Obtainable in paperback

CHAPLIN, DORA P., *The Privilege of Teaching,* Morehouse

CLARK, MARJORIE, *Methods of Teaching Religion to Children,* S.P.C.K., London

BACHMAN, JOHN W., *How to Use Audio-Visual Materials,* Association Press

GENERAL (On Understanding Children)

JENKINS, SCHACTER AND BAUER, *These are Your Children,* Scott-Foresman

PARKHURST, HELEN, *Exploring the Child's World,* Appleton-Century

LOBINGIER, JOHN, *The Better Church School,* Pilgrim Press

CHAPTER EIGHT

Ways of Approach

I. THROUGH THE BIBLE

Blessed Lord, who hast caused all holy Scriptures to be written for our learning: Grant that we may in such wise hear them, read, mark, learn, and inwardly digest them, that by patience, and comfort of the holy Word, we may embrace and ever hold fast the blessed hope of everlasting life, which thou hast given us in our Saviour Jesus Christ. Amen.

"The conviction of a few Jewish peasants in a minor dependency of the great and highly civilized Roman Empire seemed to most of its citizens an extravagant folly, but persisted as the Empire, apparently so stable and permanent, fell into collapse, and outlived every other creed and philosophy of the Graeco-Roman world. The facts recorded in the Gospels do not exhaust Christianity, but they are, in the witness of St. John's Gospel, the most important part of it. To expound these facts and thought is not to teach Christianity, it is to give premises for it. It is to give more of it than was ever given to some of us in what were regarded as Christian schools. And anyone given so much has seen the Christian life, and the grounds of the Christian faith."

—Sir Richard Livingstone
[from "The Future of Education" in *On Education*, Macmillan]

We have thought about the insufficiencies of our time. We hear constantly of the condition of the world today, and can scarcely open a magazine without reading about it. If we are realistic we admit that two clouds hang over us and over our children's future—the fear of a depression, and the fear of destruction. Our children are unconsciously affected by this, and think about it more than we realize. We have seen that the only sure thing we can offer them is a growing faith in God. In a confused and materialistic civilization, what steady light can we follow? An answer is so close at hand, in almost every home, that we fail to see it; or we may have tried to follow it and have floundered in our efforts; we have forgotten the Bible.

Why, when the Bible is still a best-seller, do we remain in complacent ignorance of its message?

Part of the reason for the ignorance of the Bible manifest in the present generation is the law about religious teaching, previously referred to, and applicable to most state schools throughout America, which forbids the public school and the state university to offer any religious instruction. In twelve states the reading of the Bible is said to be required in the lower grades, twenty-four states permit it at that level. In Virginia and Texas the high schools are reported to be launching out on a limited program of religious instruction. In Wisconsin the Supreme Court has declared that the reading of the Bible (we assume this means the King James Version) to non-Protestant children makes the school an illegal place of Protestant worship. These conditions have led the churches to found their own schools, and it is in these independent institutions, not supported by public taxes, that some of the most encouraging religious teaching is done. Parents interested in the fine efforts being made in preparatory schools throughout the country should read the inspiring papers given in the symposium *The Preparatory Schools and Re-*

ligion in Our Time [1] which is the report of a symposium rep-
resenting the considered opinions of some of our finest school
leaders. There is a grave urgency about all they say, and a
rebuke for the conventional mildness of our faith.

It is not fair, however, that we parents should put the blame
entirely on the state and the schools. While good religious
teaching in the day schools would be welcomed thankfully
by many of us, the root of the matter lies in the home. The
lost inheritance of our children was brought about by the
"let-alone" methods of a vast number of parents. After a
healthy reaction against fear and fundamentalism there came
a generation reacting against the narrow theological beliefs
thrust upon them in childhood, which in the light of historical
criticism, they were later to reject. Wishing to spare their
children disillusionment, they gave them nothing at all. The
tragic result of this procedure is that not only are children
robbed of the great religious and literary heritage belonging
to this civilization, but they are deprived of the most vital
part of their education which can help them to grow to their
full spiritual stature as mature beings.

The Bible is not the record of spiritual laws that have
ceased to function. The religious experiences we find recorded
there are not really different from ours today. In the Bible
we look for, and find, meaningful guidance for our own time,
through the mighty acts of God in the history of man. The
world-shaking event in that history was God's coming in
Christ. In Bible study we can be led through a study of the
Jesus of history to the knowledge of the Christ of the church
at work in the world today. The offering of detailed studies
of the history and geography of the Bible is not enough: what
we need is a search for the purposes of God; His own activity

[1] Association Press.

is His revelation, and that activity is recorded in the Bible.

We must not be afraid of historical criticism, for that is an attempt to understand the "Library of the Grace of God" (Dean Hodge's name for the Bible) more fully than it has been possible to do before. Instead of fearing the modern viewpoint, shown by the light of the most recent scholarship, we should value the clearer setting into which we can place the events of the life of our Lord, and look more closely into the "twilight period" of the early church. It has been suggested that the new knowledge now available to us offers us an experience not unlike that of the early Christians. Men and women of today will use their own terms in which to express His character and teaching: the important thing is that we share the *intention* of those who saw the earlier light, new terms do not matter if they are authentic.

Looking back into their own childhood, many people will tell you they were originally put off by the Doré pictures in the family Bible inherited by their relations. This is understandable up to a point. Have you ever seen an unfortunate little child being entertained with these portrayals of the peoples of the earth struggling against heaven-sent calamities of flood, fire, and pestilence? They have haunted many of us in the days before picture magazines and bad movies took away some of the natural sensitivity of the human mind. A child can to some extent see why the wicked people deserved punishment, but he will agonize over the babies and animals about to suffer violent death, shown so graphically in some of the pictures.

Another reason for the neglect of the Bible may have been due to the sentimentalizing of its study in story books current in the days of our mothers, who wept over the sorrows of the saintly Elsie Dinsmore. The methods of Biblical instruction current more than a hundred years ago, would hardly be acceptable to modern pedagogy. The little Brontës knew their Bibles well, and in *Jane Eyre* one of the lesser villains, the unctious Mr. Brocklehurst, tries his hand at religious education.

"Do you read your Bible?" he asks the trembling ten-year-old heroine.

"Sometimes."

"With pleasure? Are you fond of it?"

"I like Revelation, and the Book of Daniel and Genesis and Samuel, and a little bit of Exodus, and some parts of Kings and Chronicles, and Job and Jonah."

"And the Psalms? I hope you like them?"

"No, sir."

"No? oh, shocking! I have a boy, younger than you, who knows six psalms by heart: and when you ask him which he would rather have, a ginger-bread nut to eat, or a verse of a Psalm to learn, he says: 'Oh! the verse of a Psalm! Angels sing Psalms;' says he, 'I wish to be a little angel here below;' then he gets two nuts in recompense for his infant piety."

"Psalms are not interesting," I remarked.

"That proves you have a wicked heart; and you must pray to God to change it; to give you a new and clean one: to take away your heart of stone and give you a heart of flesh."

We do not know why Jane, the child of more than a century ago, did not like the Psalms; but I do know that I was helping one of our modern children to pack her trunk for camp, and I asked her if she wanted to take her Bible, lately presented by her Sunday school, to read while she was away. The child was eight, and she was truthful. She came up to me and almost whispered, in a confidential manner: "I don't want to hurt God's feelings, but the Bible is an awfully long book, isn't it?" Try to see through the eyes of this young person of eight, and to discover whether she can help us to realize what the Bible looks like through her eyes. It is a strange-looking book to a child: it has an unusual binding, it is printed in small type, with prose and verse looking alike; it has double columns and no paragraphs, the sentences are numbered. Moreover its stately Tudor language becomes increasingly remote to ears accustomed to the limited vocabulary and cheap expressions of today. He is fortunate indeed to whom the splendid prose is made familiar in earlier years.

Old Bibles are handed down. New ones, choicely-bound, are, by dutiful godparents and relations, often given at the child's Baptism. Too often the matter ends there. In Sunday schools where Bibles are presented, as is so often the case, when the children "graduate" to another department, the policy should be a solemn resolve to work to make the Book of Books come alive in the mind of the child. At eight years old—a very usual age to receive a Bible—the child reads with a varying degree of ease. If he knows some Bible stories he will at first get pleasure from the novelty of looking them up in this new volume, then he will often grow tired, for, as we were told, "the Bible *is* an awfully long book."

Whether the eight-year-old at the time of receiving his first Bible—or when he first begins to read the Bible for himself—has already become familiar with the language and some of the stories, or whether he is a beginner in his study of the Good Book, he will surely want to know how the Bible came to be. I have yet to find the person, young or old, who is not thrilled by this story, which, well-told, is surely as poignant and exciting as any in the world.

The history of how the Bible came into its present form cannot of course be told in detail here. Briefly it should be shown that the Bible is really a library of sixty-six volumes, the most recent of them having been written at least 1800 years ago, the oldest as far back as 1200 B.C., some of them by unknown hands.

Once the children know that St. Jerome's Latin translation of the Bible, the Vulgate, which was universally used in the Middle Ages and is still the Bible of the Roman Church, was available only to the priests and educated few in the England of that time, they are ready for the stirring events surrounding the lives of the courageous men who dared denounce the use of the Latin scriptures. They, in their land of freedom, can see that the clerical tyrants were enforcing superstitions and ceremonies on an ignorant people: to combat this, John Wycliffe, a parish priest, produced an English Bible early in the fourteenth century. At this time many of the clergy were ignorant and corrupt, and the people submitted to their frauds. Printing had not been introduced into England, and although numerous copies were made, the manuscripts were able to circulate among a considerable number of wealthier people. Let them hear how those who could not afford to buy the whole manuscript would give considerable sums for a few pages, and these pages in turn would be lent out. We read of one man paying a load of hay for permission to read a portion for one hour. In these circumstances some learned what they could by heart, and our children will like to look back through the centuries at one Alice Collins who was sent to little gatherings "to recite the ten commandments and parts of the Epistles of St. Paul and Peter." Of these people John Foxe says in his *Book of Martyrs*, "Certes the zeal of those Christian days seems much superior to this of our day, and

to see the travail of them may well shame our careless times."
According to the age, you can give a more or less detailed
story of the terrible risks attached to the study of the Bible
in Wycliffe's time. An Act of Parliament forbade the circula-
tion of the scriptures in English, and finally an appeal was
made to the Pope, who imposed a penalty of excommunica-
tion; all translations of the Bible, other than the Vulgate,
were forbidden. Then came the martyrdoms, men and women
were executed for teaching their children the Lord's Prayer
and Ten Commandments in English. Possessors of the Wycliffe Bible were hunted down like wild beasts.

Before the next great version of the Bible came the discovery of printing, and the period of toiling over handwrit-
ten manuscripts was closed. Just as dullness is the unforgivable sin in teaching the Bible, so it is in teaching the history
of how our Bible came to us. The men and women who la-
bored over it and suffered for it are in their Christian fortitude as great as any who have lived. The life of William Tyndale is like a streak of light in a dark age; his earlier life and
scholarship, his deepening interest in the wonderful revelation of the love of God to man which he found in the scriptures stirred in him the indomitable resolve to make this treasure available to every man and woman in England. He argued
with the priests and made open declaration of his hope, "If
God spare me I will one day make the boy that drives the
plough know more of the Scripture than the Pope does." He
appealed to the Bishop of London for permission to do the
work of translation in his palace: the Bishop said there was
no room. In his preface later he wrote sadly, "I perceived that
not only in my Lord of London's palace, but in all England,
there was no room for attempting a translation of the Scriptures." We must let our children know of the life of exile that

followed. In 1524 Tyndale left England, never to return. The events of the rest of his life would take up too much space here, but, the plots, treacheries, the smuggling of the New Testament into barrels, bales of cloth and every way that could be devised in order to get it into England, are part of the tale. Tyndale refused to be discouraged when they burned what copies they could seize. "They did none other than I looked for," he says, "no more shall they do if they burn me also, if it be God's will that it should be so." After years of continuous opposition and plotting and betrayal, he was finally enticed from his house in a poverty-stricken German town, and imprisoned for over a year in a dungeon at the Castle of Vievorden. What more revealing words, showing the suffering and destitution of the man, can come down the centuries that this note Tyndale sent to the governor during his imprisonment:

"I beg your lordship, and that by the Lord Jesus, that if I am to remain here during the winter, you will request the procurer to be kind enough to send me from my goods which he has in his possession a warmer cap, for I suffer extremely from a perpetual catarrh, which is much increased by this cell. A warmer coat also, for that which I have is very thin; also a piece of cloth to patch my leggings—my shirts too are worn out."

Clerical influence in England was too strongly opposed to help him, and he was martyred in October, 1536, praying with his last words, "Lord, open the King of England's eyes." Three years later an English Bible lay in every English parish church. We can follow the great story with our children; let them see the humor and diplomacy of Coverdale, who although not a man of Tyndale's spiritual stature, knew how to flatter kings, and dedicated his translation to King Henry VIII and his "dearest juste wyfe," even using a picture of the King handing out the book to his bishops.

The work of these two men: Tyndale and Coverdale is substantially the basis of the King James Version, our Bible of today, which was revised in 1611 at the order of King James, for the scholars found little need of change. "Tyndale and Coverdale lived," says Dean Hodges, "at a time when the English language was spoken with such purity, simplicity and dignity as no subsequent age has ever equalled. But it was to them that these qualities were in great measure due. They determined the language in which Shakespeare and Milton wrote. . . . The translators of the King James Version had no literary ambition. . . . Herein they were in the spirit of the men whose writings they translated. . . . They had no pride of authorship. They were therefore free from many temptations to artificiality and elaboration. It was easy for them to be simple and to choose plain enduring words. . . . Not only religion but literature is the loser by any neglect of the English Bible in the education of youth. Only to read these splendid sentences, to get the cadence and melody of them, to attend to their words and phrases, pure and undefiled and chosen with unfailing skill, is to enter into the privilege of a high discipline in the art of writing. Our chief men of letters have learned their art in this school, often by the process of committing passages of these books to memory. They have perceived, from the point of view of literature, that the English Bible is the supreme English book. . . . The men who made it, like the men whose writings they translated, were intent on religion. They cared for nothing else. . . . They believed that those who read it aright would become 'wise unto salvation.' They accounted the Bible as one of the means of grace. Out of it the minister was to instruct

the people; in it the people diligently reading would find
the minister's instruction confirmed or corrected; by means
of it both minister and people would grow in grace and in
knowledge and love of God." [2]

Coming suddenly back to our century, I now quote from
an article in the *Saturday Evening Post* of September 1944,
by Dorothy Thompson: "Parents do not wish their children
to be inculcated with doctrines foreign to their own churches.
But it is perfectly possible to discover a bedrock ethical basis
common to all the faiths institutionalized in America. And
just why the peerless monument of the English language
should be banned, or all but banned, from English studies,
from primary grades through high school, is beyond my comprehension. I refer to the King James version of the Bible.
The thirteenth chapter of First Corinthians is not only one
of the greatest treatises on transcendental ethics ever penned,
but it is also one of the greatest pieces of pure literature ever
written. The greatest of the Psalms are among the greatest
pieces of pure literature ever written. The greatest of the
Psalms are among the greatest of the world's poems. The Ten
Commandments are the basis of the laws of the nations. The
Sermon on the Mount is a social document of the loftiest
beauty. And no person who is not intimately familiar with
these passages, and many others, can have any real notion of
the basis of our civilization, its laws or its ethical standards.
. . . We are rearing generations who are neither atheist nor
agnostic for either attitude involves a disagreement with something. They are simply pagans, living in a religious and ethical
void."

Professor Mary Ellen Chase gives evidence from Smith

[2] *How to Know the Bible*, p. 344, Bobbs-Merrill. Copyright 1918, 1945.
By special permission.

College: "The Bible belongs," she says, "among the noblest and most indispensable of our humanistic and literary traditions. No liberal education is truly liberal without it. Yet in the last fifty years our colleges have, for the most part, abandoned its study as literature, and our schools, for reasons not sufficiently valid, have ceased to teach, or, in many cases, even to read it to their young people. Students of English literature take for granted that a knowledge of the *Iliad*, the *Odyssey*, the *Aeneid* and the *Divine Comedy* are necessary not only for the graduate schools but for cultured and civilized life, as, indeed, they are; but most of them remain in comfortable and colossal ignorance of a book which ante-dates Dante and, in large part, Vergil by many centuries, some of which was written before Homer, and all of which has contributed more to the humanistic civilization of the Western World than have the so-called 'Classics.' " [3]

In one of our finest theological schools, a group of young men who had been accepted, all college graduates, all planning to enter the ministry, were recently given a Bible test by one of the professors. The questions were easy—some, though not all, were as simple as "What baby was found in a cradle by a stream?" and "Who sang the Magnificat?" The highest percentage, scored by a very few, was forty; one man had as low as three per cent correct answers. These, mark you, were planning to enter a religious profession.

Many parents, approaching the heads of schools free to do something to combat this ignorance, are told that the already over-crowded college preparation course leaves them no time for Bible study. We sit back and do nothing about it, while the colleges continue to give credits for less worthy subjects.

[3] *The Bible and the Common Reader,* p. 9, Macmillan. Copyright 1944. By permission.

I have found history teachers, themselves a product of the present trend, implying to their pupils that, while the Bible was a great solace to people like our Pilgrim forefathers who were facing the same elemental difficulties as the Israelites in the wilderness, this ancient collection of books, the Bible, has little bearing upon the problems of the world in which we live. While we recognize the fact that a knowledge of the Bible does not automatically produce a Christian life in the student, is he not more likely to see his place in the pageant of history if he comes to realize something of the wonder of the slow revelation of God to man in the eighteen hundred years covered by the books of the Bible? In our day we are accused, like the ancient Romans, of cultivating, not the "practice of the presence of God" but the "presence of calamity." The New Testament teaching is, "Be not afraid of them that kill the body, and after that have no more that they can do. But I will forewarn you whom ye shall fear: fear him, which after he hath killed hath power to cast into hell; yea, I say unto you, Fear him" (Luke 12:5f). Even in troubled days like these, that is all we have to fear. Instead of bewailing continually the apparent triumph of the material over the spiritual, let us get busy and see that as many people as possible are taught to understand the record of the spiritual exalting over the material; for in the Bible there are the lives of both the great and the simple lived in the presence of God. Every one of these lives, however imperfect it might be, seemed to look toward God as a central fact, and the unseen world of the spirit was never far away from them, mistaken though they often were in their interpretation of it. Here is the record of man coming nearer to God than he had ever dared to hope, and the story of people who, defeated, were nevertheless not in despair. Here we discover, too, that sinful man, in spite of his failures, continues to hunger and thirst after righteousness.

Our young people, by their own proclamation, are hungry for good teaching on the fundamentals of our faith. Students can be guided by a trained teacher to acquire these fundamentals from their Bible studies. Then they must see how they are worked out in Christian church history and know something of their practice. "What they seem to me to include," says a modern schoolmaster, "is primarily the great doctrines of God (Father, Son and Holy Spirit), the doctrine of Man, and the idea of the Church. These will include ideas of sin, judgment, suffering, creation, redemption, the kingdom of God, eternal life, etc."

Having found, then, religious reasons and literary reasons why our children should not be robbed of what has been rightly called, "the noblest monument of English prose," how shall we begin to offer it to them?

There are some excellent books on the Bible which every teacher and parent who feels a need for further guidance should read:

CHASE, MARY E., *The Bible and the Common Reader,* Macmillan

CHASE, MARY, E., *Readings from the Bible,* Macmillan

DE DIETRICH, SUZANNE, *Discovering the Bible,* Source

ANDERSON, B. W., *Rediscovering the Bible,* Study Guide: The Unfolding Drama of the Bible, Association Press

DE DIETRICH, SUZANNE, *The Witnessing Community,* Westminster. (Study Guide from Seabury Press)

RICHARDSON, ALAN, *A Preface to Bible Study,* Westminster

DENTAN, R. C., *The Holy Scriptures,* Seabury

PARKER, PIERSON, *Inherit the Promise,* Seabury

KEE, H. C., and YOUNG, F. W., *Understanding the New Testament,* Prentice-Hall

Ways of Approach—The Bible

ANDERSON, B. W., *Understanding the Old Testament,* Prentice-Hall
BECK, D. M., *Through the Gospels to Jesus,* Harper

AIDS TO TEACHING THE BIBLE

MILLER, RANDOLPH C., *Biblical Theology and Christian Education,* Scribners
SMITHER, E., *The Use of the Bible with Children,* Abingdon
LACE, O. JESSIE, *Teaching the Old Testament,* Seabury

INVALUABLE BACKGROUND MATERIAL

BOUQUET, A. C., *Everyday Life in New Testament Times,* Scribners
HEATON, E. W., *Everyday Life in Old Testament Times,* Scribners
JOHNSON, SHERMAN E., *Jesus in His Homeland,* Scribners
(Ask your minister about modern translations and paraphrases like those of J. B. Phillips).

The following list suggests a few "shorter Bibles," or Bible stories from the King James Version:

5–7 years *The Little Children's Bible,* Macmillan
7–9 years *The Jesus Story,* Illustrated by Maud and Miska Petersham, Doubleday
7–11 years *The Older Children's Bible,* Macmillan
From 5 up: *The Children's Bible,* Helicon Press, Baltimore. $2.50 cloth bound and $1.00 paper covers. Modern pictures, very good.
From about 11 years *The Children's Bible,* Sherman and Kent, Scribners. With illustrations
The Book of Books, Sypherd, W. O.,—Knopf
From 6 years up to 14 or older Barnhart, Nancy, *The Lord is My Shepherd,* Scribners

A very beautiful book pictured in Bible lands. Well-told stories, and extracts are given from the King James version.

Children and Religion

N.B. In the monthly magazine, *Highlights for Children* I re-tell an Old Testament story in each number. It is a good magazine, and it is sometimes wise to have the Bible story included in a book of fun, games, and non-religious stories. A descriptive folder may be obtained from **Garry C. Myers**, Ph.D., *Highlights for Children*, Honesdale, Pa.

D.P.C.

While these editions are helpful for many, others will demand stories "From the real Bible, Daddy, the one that looks like yours," and because they love to imitate, scorn the substitute.

The more recent translations of the Bible into modern English, while they are not of greater literary value, are sometimes very useful for reading with older children, especially those who have only just "discovered" the Bible, and are greatly puzzled by the Elizabethan prose. For these a "Parallel Testament" is often a great help. There is of course the Revised Standard Version which is widely read.

From the outset we should be clear that there is no magic formula, no set rule, as to what Bible teaching a child should have at a given age. There is, in fact, much disagreement among wise and earnest teachers of religion, as to what should be taught first. Some of them, while giving excellent reasons for their theories, are not very practical. An entire book, *How to Tell Bible Stories* (Scribners), by Louise Seymour Houghton, was written to defend the Old-Testament-First idea. The author argues that there is much similarity between the Hebrew mind and the mind of childhood, and that the right teaching of Old Testament stories can bring the sense of God to a child as part of his second nature. She points out that while there are stumbling-blocks and perplexities, these stories, well told, can put into concrete form abstract truth to be interpreted by the imagination. Mrs. Houghton points out that the Hebrew in which they were originally written has no abstract words, they are all concrete, as a little child's are, and this makes them eminently suitable for the young child. At three years old she would give an outline, at five "a simple unfolding of the spiritual meaning," and proceed through more advanced historical work to the study of ethics and philosophy at sixteen or so. The book is written with such integrity that it is well worth reading. Even if one cannot go all the way with its thesis, it is a splendid aid to Old Testament story-telling.

Every parent and teacher should try to turn himself into a good story-teller—narrative is indispensable.

In *Children's Religion* [4] there appeared in the fall and spring of 1946–1947 a series of cartoons by Jeanette Perkins Brown, in which she tries to teach "When a Story is a Story." Some of it may seem elementary, but if we test our narrative ability as applied to the stories we tell our children, we shall not always pass the test. We are told to divide the story thus:

> Introduction . . . (It arouses interest and curiosity at once)
> Action . . . (It *goes* somewhere)
> Conflict. Suspense . . . (Difficulties present themselves)
> Climax . . . (Matters reach a crisis)
> Conclusion . . . (Way is now open for solution of all problems)
> Listeners Relax . . . (And initial curiosity is satisfied. Minds are at ease)

These articles have now been incorporated into an excellent book, an invaluable possession for teachers, parents, and the clergy. It is called *The Storyteller in Religious Education,*

[4] A monthly magazine published by the Pilgrim Press.

by Jeanette Perkins Brown (Pilgrim Press, 1951). It has fine bibliographies, and many illustrations of the types of story suited to the different levels of age. The art of the story-teller is indispensable to all who teach, and I urge the use of this book for everyone who wants to increase the effectiveness of his work.

Those who prefer to read to their children from one of the good collections of Bible stories, will find suggestions in Chapter Ten, on Books.

Personally, I can see rocks ahead for the average child if the parents decide to tell nothing but Old Testament stories. Most Sunday schools tell both Old and New Testament stories in the earlier grades, so that puts Sunday school out of bounds if this advice is to be carried out literally. And how can the child participate in the great festivals of the Christian church without some knowledge of what he is celebrating? Is he not to have the stories surrounding Christmas, Palm Sunday, Easter? All these festivals, we believe, he can take part in on the different levels of his maturing life. If he goes to church with his parents, will he not be puzzled over New Testament references there? I am sure most advocates of this method do not mean to neglect the New Testament—rather are they trying to preserve it for the time when it can be more fully understood, but there have been many instances of the over-stressing of the Old Testament *to the neglect of the New,* and this has been found to account for the sub-Christian or even un-Christian ideas of God held by many young people. Surely the young child needs the comfort and the joy of knowing that Jesus came to show us what God is like, and to hear a few stories about Him: if they are given the right guidance, this will not be overdone. And they can also have all the glory of the Old Testament that they can appreciate.

We must, however, remain keenly alert to the danger of presenting a hotch-potch of Bible stories to young children; it is better to err on the side of too few than too many. We have referred in other places to the danger of telling one story after another, hoping piously that they have been assimilated, and not waiting to have them "told back." We offer meat that is too strong, and there is confusion. A kindergarten child with a new French governess known, not surprisingly, as "Madame" went home from Sunday school recently and announced that she'd heard "a lovely story about Madame and Eve." Another household in the same neighborhood heard a first grade child sing, "Heck, the herald angels sing" with great fervor throughout the Christmas season.

Of little use is the care given to the choice of stories told in Sunday school if just any book of Bible stories is picked up and read at home. How can God be kind, if He wanted to drown the whole world, is the question in the child's mind, and how can He be kind if he wanted Abraham to kill Isaac? We can sympathize with a six-year-old child I know who was heard confiding to her five-year-old sister; "Sometimes I like God, and sometimes—I don't." Perhaps it is unnecessary to say, conversely, that the parents should discover what is being done at Sunday school!

Assuming that we as parents have equipped ourselves with the beginnings of wise Bible study in the books mentioned, that we have read to the child from the King James Version in some form, choosing stories that seem right for his age level, well-told stories of the childhood of Jesus fit in very well here, for they help to give the background of Palestinian life and free the child's imagination for much that is not told in the Bible itself. Little children do a great deal of reasoning. I was talking about the boyhood of Jesus to a class of six-year-olds when one young philosopher, after deep thought, said in a puzzled voice, "But when Jesus went to school, did he learn about *himself?*" This set everyone else thinking, and helped us all. What were the stories Jesus probably heard? They were much pleased to find that he heard the ones they knew themselves, about Abraham, and Samuel, and David. The little boy who had asked the first question looked very serene before he went home, and volunteered with a happy grin: "And I expect Jesus used to slide down the mountains with the other boys." This was something he could very well appreciate.

In the earlier part of the book we have suggested the kind of interest the child is likely to have at different levels. We saw that in first and second grade we have a good opportunity to teach to the six- and seven-year-olds something of Palestinian life and the customs of the East. This prepares the way for what seems a very important but frequently overlooked fact in our Bible teaching: the difference between the Oriental and the Western mind. Educated natives of Syria tell us that they have often heard the people of their country, to this day, speak of angels and the messages they have brought them in dreams. Mr. Ribhany, a native of Syria, says: "The Oriental's manner of speech has been that of a worshipper and not that of a business man or an industrial worker in the modern Western sense. To the Syrian of today, as to his ancient ancestor, life with all its activities and cares, revolves around a religious center. . . . He has no secular language. . . . When you ask a Syrian about his business he will not answer, 'We are doing well at present,' but 'God is giving bounteously.' To one starting on a journey the phrase is not 'Take good care of yourself,' but 'Go, in the keeping and protection of God.' " Miss Streibert quotes him (this writer) as saying in a lecture that "the Oriental does not speak in literal terms and that he assumes no one will understand him so; he speaks with a certain fearlessness and assurance of being right. He would say, 'The spirit of the Lord came to me saying, 'Son of man, Prophesy,' never as the more precise and cautious Anglo-Saxon might say, 'It seemed to me like the spirit of God, and I'll do my best in my poor way.' " [5]

Simple memory work, carefully chosen, can begin at this age, and with the repetition of stories from the Bible itself it has probably begun unconsciously. In families, in classes, or among groups of friends, dramatization is a valuable way of learning and impressing what has been learned. It is impossible to lay down the law as to what every grade should have at a certain age. Every district, with its varying background and achievements, must work out something best suited to its needs. Almost never can you hand a course to a teacher and say, "This is fine: proceed exactly as it says here."

During the past two decades there is hardly a denomination of the Christian Church which has not revised its curriculum material in a drastic way. The better material produced by individual publishers has also been revised; the best is in a constant state of revision every few years as suggestions come in from the field.

The Christian Education Departments of the Episcopal Church and of The Presbyterian Church in U.S.A. in particular have spent millions of dollars and have big staffs working constantly on the production of materials for both children and their parents; also for other adults, of course.

The results of these big efforts have been varied. Three positive ones should be noted: There is far more adult study going on; more well-educated people are taking the teaching of religion seriously and work hard at it; the "Family Service" in

[5] Ribhany, *Syrian Christ,* Houghton Mifflin Co.

different forms shows that parents realize the need for whole families to worship together. They see the folly of the fragmentation which was fashionable for a long period, where every member of the family worshipped, as it were, in a separate little cell.

No matter how much money we spend, and how much concentrated effort goes into the spreading of the Gospel in our land and beyond it, Christian family life, and the effect of the parents' beliefs and lives upon the new generation will always be of central importance: Christian family life and teaching will exert a deeper influence than that "crowded hour of glorious life" which we call "Sunday school." At the moment we need both, especially for those children who receive no Christian influence or instruction in their homes.

Tragically, there is still much very bad material being produced, often written by those who do not know children, least of all modern children. These courses have just as much a part in "the seduction of the innocent" as bad work without a pious cloak; they are produced with money-making in view and with little or no understanding of the harm they are doing. Some of them talk to our vigorous children as though they were little replicas of those who lived in the Victorian era. Others are so weak and sugary in their theology and Bible teaching that no wonder the pupils reject the Church and everything belonging to it as soon as they have any degree of independence. You will find few books in our public schools like these, they have neither religious nor intellectual integrity.

Those in local churches responsible for choosing curriculum materials should write to their national or regional Board of Christian Education (your pastor will give you the address) and find out what is available. If you wish to use what is published by other denominations, find out what is being sold through a big central book store and publishing house. Plan your work over a cycle of several years so that subjects are not repeated. Time is short, use it well!

Many schools eventually evolve their own courses, and the leader often furnishes mimeographed outlines to the teacher. A typical lesson used in the Outline Scheme on p. 104 reads as follows:

UNIT I. *THE PREPARATION*

LESSON III

MOSES—(Founder of the Religion and Nation of Israel).
AIM: To show something of the character and genius of Moses. Above all to show *what he discovered about God,* how he relied upon God and stayed close to him; *(hence his great success as a leader)*; how he entered into a promise with God and led the nation to do so, making them feel "a holy nation," and his fight against idolatry. Moses found that he could tell the people what God wanted them to do, because he listened for God's voice. The older ones can be led to feel all this, but at the end of the lesson leave them all ready to go on with the quest—he taught them that *God alone can be depended on*—but—how far is Man in his search for God at the point we have reached? The following shows us:

Moses' God "was a God who intervened to save His people by mighty acts of deliverance and called men to be His instruments in such a saving; a jealous God also tolerating no rivals, demanding utter loyalty and obedience; a God of fire, storm and volcano;—blazing forth in anger at rebellion; yet a God who cared for Israel, and in the midst of punishment remembered mercy; . . . who desired to be worshipped through rites and institutions, but most of all required righteousness; a God who took thought for the poor and oppressed, who provided food and drink for His people, but as His chief gift imparted to them the knowledge of His holy will." [6]

IMPORTANT: What was missing in the discovery of God as far as Man has gone in his search—that is as far as we have discovered in these lessons? Lead them to find out that the missing thing—or one of them—was the discovery that God cared for *all Peoples*—because He is the *God of Heaven and Earth*, not just of *one nation*. How long do they think Man will be before he discovers this? Jacob found that God could be in more than one place, but the Israelites haven't yet found that He belongs to more than one nation.

Suggestions for starting the lesson. Most of the children know a collection of various facts and stories of Moses. If you are not on your guard the younger ones will use up the time telling you how much they know about his adventures in the bulrushes. Assume that they know this story—recall it if you wish, and if any child does not know it take down the name and lend him a book about it. Older ones will try to dwell on the details of the Ten Plagues. Tell this first as an outline story: e.g. "I expect you all know how, after Joseph died in Egypt, the Israelites (or 'Children of Israel' as they are sometimes called, because you know Jacob changed his name to Israel) had lots of children and grandchildren, and lived on in Egypt for hundreds of years, until there were so many of them that a cruel Pharaoh was afraid they might over-run his land, and he made them slaves. They were overworked and beaten and had a terrible time. They wished some strong leader could help them." Then go on to a brief outline of Moses' upbringing, his flight, and his *call from God*.

[6] Fleming James, *Personalities of the Old Testament*, p. 42, Scribners.

Who else had a call from God to lead his people? (Abraham). Tell about the flight from Egypt and the forty years in the Wilderness. Why do they think it was good to spend forty years wandering? What did Moses teach the people in that time? (Leadership was developed and a new generation was born. The people were trained in the arts of war. Laws were made and enforced. The people were prepared physically, politically and spiritually for the task of reconquering Caanan). Please have the children tell *you* this as far as possible. Make them think. What would they have done in the circumstances? The stories of Moses are full of human traits common to us all. They can, for example, appreciate how Moses felt when God's call came to him and he pleads: "I am slow of speech, and of a slow tongue." (See Exodus 4:10). And again, the repeated "murmuring" against their leader and "Why did you bring us out of the Land of Egypt to die?" and the patience and fortitude of Moses are readily understood.

Read the whole story in the Bible (References follow) and reproduce it in language suitable to the grade. May I remind you how very much smaller a child's vocabulary is than an adult's—it is so easy to have him miss a vital point by misunderstanding one word.

MEMORY: For those ready to memorize for you at home (there are a few in each grade) choose verses from Deut. 31 and 34—e.g. verse 6 in Chapter 31 and verse 10 in Chapter 34.

How many of the pupils know the Ten Commandments, even in a shortened version?

TEACHING MATERIAL

ADAPTABLE FOR ALL: Photographs of famous pictures of Moses will be available from the Museum of Fine Arts and can be passed around.

(Grade 4 level.) George Hodges, *Garden of Eden,* pp. 47–62, obtainable from public libraries.

F. James, *Personalities of the Old Testament*—excellent for the teacher's own reading in the character, limitations and genius of Moses;

M. Magnuson, *Bible in the Building of Life,* pupil's book 1, pp. 166, mid. 19;

Flight and Fahs, *Moses,* whole book, (Grade 5 upwards);

Mary Chapin White, *The Old Testament and You,* Part IV, pp. 57–62;

A. G. Baldwin, *Drama of Our Religion,* pp. 47–53.

BIBLICAL REFERENCES

(See A. Graham Baldwin's *The Drama of Our Religion*)

Hebrews Enslaved ....Exodus 1: 8–22
Birth of Moses ....Exodus 2: 1–10
Moses' Flight ....Exodus 2: 11–15
Hebrews Enslaved ....Exodus 5
Moses Called ....Exodus 3: 1–17
Plagues ....Exodus 7, 8, 9, 10 and 11
Passover ....Exodus 12: 1–14
Crossing the Red Sea ....Exodus 14
Thanksgiving ....Exodus 15: 1–19
Ten Commandments..Exodus 19: 20—Exodus 20: 24
Golden Calf ....Exodus 32
Tabernacle ....Exodus 40
Spies Sent Out ....Numbers 13: 1–2; 17–33
Death of Moses ....Deut. 31: 1–8; 24: 1–12

The curriculum is best based, from at least the third grade, on a five- or six-year plan, so that each pupil before leaving will have had at least an outline of the essentials, and we hope be stimulated to look for more. Here again it is impossible to dictate a hard-and-fast rule, for in some districts church school goes on through High School age, in others the majority of the young people leave in the seventh or eighth grade and go away to boarding-school. These preparatory schools may or may not have a course of sacred studies: we have already mentioned the splendid work being done in some. A fairly common plan is for the preparatory school to offer an Old Testament course, followed by an intensive study of one of the gospels (frequently St. Mark), a year of church history, and a final one on theology and ethics with ample time for discussion and for application to life. Ambitious, you say? Yes, but *with good teachers,* how much better it is than to sit back and do nothing!

In those churches where the children attend public school —and these are in the majority—the serious and urgent responsibility at present lies with the home and the church. It is generally conceded that most of the losses from which the church suffers are due to the fact that the dogmas taught in childhood and never applied to life and the arrogant declarations of opinion to which the children have listened, or teaching so vague and watered-down as to be an insult to growing intelligence, have been rejected in later life. We must try to teach what may be verified in maturity. This is not a new idea, and how much longer shall we fail to act upon it?

In the year 735 A.D. the Venerable Bede was lying on his deathbed, feebly dictating to his scribes a translation of St. John's Gospel. He refused to rest when requested, and the reason he gave for trying to finish his work was, "I don't want my boys to read a lie, or to work to no purpose after I am gone." Is it not true that we who teach should have our eyes looking towards the need of tomorrow?

If there is available for a child neither a good Sunday school where accredited Biblical scholarship is presented to the understanding of childhood and of youth, nor a course in the day school, the responsibility does indeed lie with double weight upon his parents. I wish we could start some national concern existing to help parents, perhaps by mail, who live in outlying districts or for other reasons have this difficulty. Many of them admit with honesty that they earnestly wish to train their children, but belong to the generation that was given so little. Even with a genuine religious faith of their own, parents frequently own to being at a loss as to how to teach religion to a little child; the years go on, and they do nothing at all. In one state a remarkable rural mission was conducted in that way; mimeographed lessons were sent by mail, and books suggested, while its energetic founder visited outlying farmhouses at certain seasons of the year. After a time the children ran a magazine of their own, and in great numbers were led to be really effective members of the local churches when they grew up.

With the right books for both parents and children, with a love of children and religion and the desire to teach, professional aid, though often useful, is not necessary. It is perfectly possible for a child to receive the beginnings of a good religious education at home, and since in any case the church or school would have a limited amount of time for this vital work, the task comes back to us, as parents, every time. The parents may be set on fire by their own convictions and have caught the contagious enthusiasm of the books we have suggested, but we had better be warned from the beginning that everything will conspire to prevent our carrying out these good resolutions, unless we happen to live in one of those rare households where there is adequate domestic help. Childhood illnesses, social obligations, overwork—all these muster against us and tend to detract us from our goal. We have seen that bedtime is often the logical hour, but again we must be on the alert and not let the child get the impression that God is a cosy bedtime guardian not much interested in everyday affairs. Vacations can be utilized if we care enough, and may be the only time we can give our children the priceless memory of our having read something together *as a family.* Another important fact to have in mind, however, is the awareness that as the child grows the family unit is generally too small to maintain the fine standards you are trying to teach, and it is essential to look for larger Christian social experiences and opportunities for service, bridging the age-old gap between contemplation and action.

One answer to the much reiterated plea of "no time" which comes from the overcrowded parents of our overburdened modern children comes from the Fessenden School, in Newton, Massachusetts, where they are so determined that their boys (who leave them in the eighth grade) shall not go from them, without at least an outline knowledge of the Bible, that they have published two books of readings from the Old and New Testaments, one for every day of the school year, giving the events chronologically as far as possible, and each reading taking three or four minutes, all from the King James Version. Unfortunately these are no longer in print, but I recommend Katharine Fessenden's new book, *The Old Testament Story* (Adam to Jonah) written especially for children eight to ten years. It is beautifully illustrated from the old masters.[7]

A further widespread need, in which we as parents and teachers can do much to help, is the necessity for more memorizing of some of the passages of the Bible and other great

[7] Published by Henry Z. Walck, Inc.

literature. At the previously-mentioned Atlantic City conference, from which I have quoted freely because it enables
us to listen in to some of the best academic and religious
thought about the young people of today, Norman B. Nash,
retired Bishop of Massachusetts, speaking in approval of his
colleagues' plea for more memorizing of the Bible, said, "I'm
afraid we have gone a long, long way beyond any healthy
reaction against an exaggerated use of memory work. We have
almost forgotten the human memory, and depend upon the
reference book to do it all. But what the phrases, the golden
phrases, of the great Book can mean in human life, when
you're far from the Book! How badly we prepare our pupils
for spiritual crises, if we do not fill their minds and memories
with the classic utterances of religious faith, of confidence in
God, and trust in our Lord, Jesus Christ." You can hear that
plea from wise teachers all over the country. Children memorize very naturally from an early age. To begin with, such
selections as are found in Elizabeth Orton Jones' *Small Rain*
(or some of her other titles) can be readily learned by the child,
simply by having them read to him. We need great stars to
steer by, great thought to help offset the vulgarity of today's
language, something to reach for when we discover life is "too
big for our own telling," some light that will shine steadily
when sorrow has extinguished every other lamp. I must confess this to be one department of home education where I
believe a little bribery does not come amiss.

Chaplains from both world wars have come back wondering bitterly "where men acquired their ignorance of the
Christian religion." There is nothing more challenging than
their reports of the indifference and ignorance found in the
forces. A hundred of these chaplains from one denomination
signed a petition calling upon their church to do something

about its system of religious education. One returned chaplain, Dr. Robert Curry, says that four convictions have come out of the long thought he has given to the problem: [8]

> 1. As Christians and teachers of the Christian faith, we have lost contact with the greatest truth of our religion— our belief in a Personal God who revealed Himself supremely in the life and person of Jesus Christ. What we have done is to take the teachings of Jesus and divorce them from the God-Man . . . It results in the teaching of a code of ethical culture without the deep roots of a vital sense of the Presence of God.
>
> 2. Before we can do this we must become converted men and women ourselves.
>
> 3. We must place the teaching of religion back where it belongs, a *subject of importance* in the school curriculum. (Later on he says, "In academic importance the Christian faith rates behind physical education and domestic science.")
>
> 4. The need to rid ourselves of any misconception of the word "liberal" and of the fear which many of us have of the word "dogmatic."

I have heard Dr. Curry, when speaking to parents, cite the instance of a conversation with a college student, who was convinced, in spite of what is now happening in the world, that man will pull himself up by his own bootstraps and needs no help from God. This girl is typical of thousands, and they can defend their position in good humanistic logic. "No ethical code," said Dr. Curry, "even though coming from Jesus Himself, will stand by itself. We must return to the basic tenets of our religion—religion about God the Father, God

[8] Compiled from *The Preparatory Schools and Religion in Our Times,* pp. 3–6, Association Press.

the Son, and God the Holy Spirit, with all that this implies.
The comprehensive definition of Christian education once
given by Dr. Adelaide Case, and quoted at this same conference is as follows:

> "Christian education is the effort to make available for
> our generation—children, young people, and adults—the
> accumulated treasures of Christian life and thought, in such
> a way that God in Christ may carry on His redemptive work
> in each human soul and in the common life of man."
>
> The greatest of these accumulated treasures is the Bible,
> and the concerted efforts of home, church and school must
> be directed to give them a knowledge of it. Once having
> offered them the best that is available through the guidance
> of modern scholarship, we must then remind ourselves that
> we are setting out, not especially to make the child think
> for himself, nor to have him think like anyone else, but in
> the hope "that the mind of Christ may be in him."

We need to establish, not the authority of God in any one
place in the Bible, but the authority of the Bible *as a whole,*
and to direct our study of man's groping journey in the Old
Testament towards the illumination of the gospels in the life
of Jesus Christ.

In all our study of the suggested books and of the pros and
cons of teaching methods, we must never lose sight of the central fact—that we are teaching *a way of life.* We have seen that
while the acquisition of Biblical information, of history and
geography, is helpful to a degree, it must not detract us from
the core of teaching. The important thing we want our children to do is to learn to see Jesus as His contemporaries saw
Him, to know Him in His glorified humanity as the Risen
Lord, and to be touched with a conviction so great that it
changes their lives.

Weekly digests and the din of the radio or television will not answer our questions. All is *not* well with our world. Let us lead our children to learn of God's will for the world, that, like St. Paul "They may stand in the evil day, and having done all, to stand."

CHAPTER NINE

Ways of Approach

II. THROUGH PICTURES, MUSIC AND POETRY

"The beautiful is inseparably united to the good and the true, and the human mind that has not developed the experience of it has failed to realize the whole of reality, for the very nature of the sense of beauty is such that through it we gain a clearer concept of the other two values. The history of the race has shown that at the height of materialistic success, the desire for artistic enjoyment has been a potent factor in bringing a people back to the higher ideals which underlie a peaceful intercourse between nations. . . . A sense of beauty is as vital to the complete existence of the race as is the sense of justice."

—HERBERT S. LANGFELD
[*The Aesthetic Attitude* (Harcourt Brace)]

"Most people would be richer and stronger to resist the many wasteful distractions and destructive elements of modern life if their education had given them a profounder experience of the artistic or religious creations dealing with the position of man in the natural and spiritual universe."

—ROBERT ULICH
[*Fundamentals of Democratic Education* (American Book Co.)]

We now reach the place where angels, artists, scholars, and other people of consequence fear to tread. There is much controversy between the exponents of art and religion, and we hesitate to trespass into their realms of advanced aesthetics and philosophy. We retreat to our own ground, that of the religious education of the young, and there we may venture to put forward a few ideas.

We cannot remind ourselves too often that it is impossible to separate religious education from education as a whole. We want all education to be religious in the sense that it should contribute to the enlargement of the spirit. The sickness of this civilization is largely due to the lack of the experience of transcendence—"a going beyond"—there is little belief in anything except that which is seen, which is material power and prosperity. The word "mystical" to most people means a vague, perhaps even superstitious, escape from unconscious fears. The Greeks were, in certain phases of their civilization, acutely aware of the need, in the growth of the human soul, for what they called "a sense of wonder."

In considering the place of art in the religious life of the child, we must from the beginning be clear as to whether we mean appreciation, the ability to apprehend in some measure the work of artists—pictures, music, poetry—or the creation of works of art: it is with the former that we are chiefly concerned, for the techniques of artistic production lie beyond the scope of this book. "Education," said A. Graham Baldwin at the Atlantic City conference mentioned in the previous chapter, "must bring students face to face with the fact that we are God's creatures, that God is our Father. It should lead them into a vital relationship with God. . . . If religion is a combination of thought and feeling, our task as educators should be to aim at nothing less than setting before our students *the best in thought and feeling that man has experienced in the past, and can experience today*. Moreover, if religion is the attitude toward the power that we believe to be influencing our life and determining our destiny, then all that takes place in the classroom—in every classroom—and all that happens outside of the classroom affects and modifies our attitude toward God and our way of living which grows out of this attitude. Our study of science, of history, of art, of mathematics—all has its influence. Thus, in a very real sense, directly or indirectly, every course of study constitutes part of the general process of religious education." My plea is for a closer co-ordination between "the *best* in thought and feeling that man has experienced," and for an attempt to offer it to them.

We are rearing a generation of children who cannot use the resources for happiness and growth that lie within themselves. They are losing the power to create from within. We are not condemning movies as a whole; they have as we know come to stay. They can be raised to a high standard, for their production is an art in itself. It is when "going to the movies" is regarded as the one panacea for that most tragic of known ills—boredom—that the situation becomes tragic. What shall we do this free afternoon? We must go to the movies. Which movie? Very often, just *any* movie, for we must be entertained. Small families, and the predominance of apartment life, have all helped to bring about this trend. One of the great contributions made by the many good summer camps is to give our children at least a taste of the satisfying experience of writing and acting their own plays in small groups, and generally testifying to the fact that human beings still have the resourcefulness and humor to do these things. In the old days of larger families and smaller communities, this was a normal part of social life: of course amateur dramatics go on, but it is a pity we cannot make them a less self-conscious and much rehearsed form of recreation.

And what shall we do with that spare half-hour? Turn on the radio or television! Is that a crime? Of course not. Here again we have the possibilities of a fine educative and recreative force in modern life: we can hear drama, debate and great music, or we can relax to lighter music—all this not available in other generations. The tragedy is that television and radio have become a drug, a never-ending conglomeration of sound to a frightening percentage of the population of this country: silence would mean they would have to think. They have lost the desire to think: turn on the radio or television. We are being doped into a cow-like immobility. As with the movies, experts in juvenile delinquency say that they do not think parents fully appreciate the harm done by the continuous "listening-in" to crime stories on the radio, reinforced by more crime stories in the movies. Discriminating youngsters, with plenty of other mental and emotional food to counterbalance this unwholesome diet, learn to laugh at them: I have had eleven-year-olds proclaim these crime stories to be much less "dopey" than the regular "soap operas." Many of the healthy-minded will improvise a skit for you, in the best manner of the underworld, "See here, buddy, I'll be taking you for a ride" style, between clenched teeth. These are probably not the children whose personality is being warped by this fare. It is the unsuccessful child, the mentally-starved, perhaps lonely child, who wants to be thought well of by the gang, to be tough and heroic, who digests all these false standards. Although the title may be "crime doesn't pay," a good many young people who are bright enough can prove to you that—in these stories—it does.

Children and Religion

In a very frank talk with one of my own children, she volunteered that for sometime, in order to listen to a certain mystery program, she had rushed through her homework, or interrupted it with various excuses, and for a while done poor work on this account. These programs had obviously cast a spell over her, and when we decided together to limit them to two a week, at any rate during the school year, she looked much relieved, as though she had wanted somebody to take hold of the situation. The reading of good mystery stories also seems to help satisfy the desire for this type of entertainment. On the whole I think that we parents are lazy. We are apt to get caught by the tide of contemporary opinion, and to take the line of least resistance to these difficulties; most parents I have talked to find the "compromise" method best. It is a question of demand and supply. If we allow those whose values are purely commercial to mold our children's taste, we shall all suffer.

Then there is the vexed question of the comic books. Statistics have been made of their reported readership in big representative areas of this country. About 88% of children between the ages of eight and ten years buy comic books; 91% between eleven and thirteen years; 75% between fourteen and sixteen years, and 52% between the age of eighteen and twenty. These readers buy between one and ten books a week, which vary very much in quality, from the innocuous to the bad.

Opportunists have seized upon the familiar technique of the funny magazine, and instead of "blood-and-thunder" offer Bible narratives, some in vulgar style, some sentimental. I have not yet found any well-drawn ones, and wish I could. American History and propaganda about the United Nations all followed in the same guise, as did the educational efforts of different political parties. Some, doing rather better, made use of the familiar style to try to improve the attitude of children towards other races, while famous books are "done down" into these quickly assimilated forms. Much of it is probably harmless, some of it fairly good. The trouble comes, as it so often does, when this sham stuff is offered as a substitute for the real, and the reader develops such a taste for it that he has patience for nothing else: why should he use his mind, when all this is offered for his entertainment and can be consumed without mental effort? No wonder a friend of mine who teaches at a famous university in this country ventured the suggestion at a faculty meeting that students should be able to read and write before having degrees conferred upon them.

But isn't it better, people will say, to learn that way than not at all? It is true that many children now seem to have been reduced to the state of not being able to learn anything unless it is dressed up in comic-book style. One minister tried to rally the nation's church school-staffs by pointing out that the strong heroes of these poor stories are what please the children, and that while the pitiful watered-down renderings of Bible stories, for example, are offered, you cannot blame the children for preferring strong meat. The real danger lies—as with poor movies, the radio, television, and advertisements —in the lulling to sleep of the higher powers of appreciation and criticism latent in our children, and of the frightening total of wasted hours during the most formative years. In the name of common sense, if we wish to have any decent intellectual standard in this country, we must try to stem the tide of poor taste. For the past few years we can again look with gratitude to the summer camps which absorb so many of our children: they seem to be making a united effort by asking at the beginning of the session that no comic books be sent, following the request with the statement that the harm is not so serious when one child reads one book, but begs us to view what the situation is when fifty children read and lend fifty books.

"It's all part of the American scene," we hear, "and I don't want my children to be different." Then they proceed to tell you the number of fine men and women who have grown up unscathed by this habit. Of course there are thousands of exceptions to every rule; the harm is done to the many whose backgrounds are impoverished in any case, and we increase the penury by allowing their helplessness to be fair game for a huge national income.

Parents and others who care about the effect of Crime Comics and similar products should read:

Seduction of the Innocent, Frederic Wertham, M.D., Rinehart

The following pamphlets are also important:

Television: "How to Use it Wisely with Children," Josette Frank
    From Child Study Association of America, 132 East 74th Street, New York 21, N.Y. (Their whole list of parent and teacher pamphlets is excellent.)
"Comics, Radio, Movies—and Children," Josette Frank
    From Public Affairs Committee, Inc., 22 East 38th Street, New York 16, N.Y.

America has more fine books for children than any country in the world. If children are offered the best ones—those that are attractive and interesting and open up new vistas of imagination—ones that according to their divers tastes they honestly enjoy, and if they are given them early, you have given them a standard, and although they may have a temporary taste for the "funnies," they are less likely to have a craving for them, and they are likely to pall very soon, especially when enough of the good fare is left within reach.

Parents will find attractive children's books in the Junior sections of the public libraries. Librarians find that once the young are interested in their division of the work, they become enthusiastic patrons. A further invaluable resource is a catalogue called *Best Books for Children,* put out by R. R. Bowker Co., 62 West 45th Street, New York. It is renewed annually and draws its descriptions from the best libraries. Find the right book for the right child, and you have the beginning of happy reading.

The fact is that we underestimate the children's sensibility. If what you offer is simple, you can give them what is high and deep, and will find them sensitive to it in both thought and feeling. But you must begin early. If you begin late you will have to go slowly, and good habits often start, as suggested above, by offering a book that is "just right," and in line with the child's interests at that time. This brings us back to our reason for starting the reading of the Bible early in the child's life. "It is no wonder," says Walter Russell Bowie in the little book, *The Bible,* previously mentioned, "that its beauty of spirit and beauty of word have been the root from which have sprung many flowerings.

"To the inspiration of the Bible is due such great music as . . . Handel's *Messiah* and the chorales of Bach. . . . To this same inspiration we owe the incomparable loveliness of the Madonnas and the paintings of the birth in Bethlehem, and the Holy Family, and the visit of the Wise Men, with which Fra Angelico and Perugino and Raphael and others without number have filled the art galleries of the world. And to this inspiration of the Bible we owe the influences in English prose and poetry so manifold that no brief catalogues could name them."

Parents who are themselves specialists in one form or another of the fine arts, will, consciously or unconsciously, have communicated some of their taste and enthusiasm to the children. These parents, and those who have already found a satisfactory way of setting the child's feet in the right aesthetic direction, had better skip this part of the chapter.

Having ventured to express the hope that the "funnies" might be kept at a minimum, we had better consider what we can give the child instead. In some homes there are so many good picture books and pictures available that with complete unselfconsciousness the standard of taste is built up and absorbed. In others there is so little of the best that, if the child is ever to acquire artistic appreciation, it will have to come from outside the home. At home we can provide some of the fine picture books available—there were never so many to chose from—and once again, when we buy books of Bible stories, we must avoid Christmas-card angels and depictions of an effeminate Jesus in a long white nightgown. The simplicity of the old masters—for example, the Nativity pictures of Fra Angelico are loved by most children if they have not had the overdose of sentimental pictures beforehand. I believe the best religious pictures for children are these primitives and also the modern ones that leave much room for the child's imagination. For example, the modern illustrations in *Children's Bible* (Helicon Press) see p. 129 are enough to stir the child's imagination, without daring to enforce our adult conception of detail. In a greater way the sacramental strength of a Fra Angelico can be felt.

A helpful book for parents is Annis Duff's *Bequest of Wings,*

subtitled, *A Family's Pleasures with Books.* Although it errs
a little on the "precious" side, it is full of valuable material.
The main theme is on the choice and enjoyment of books for
children, but two other chapters tie in with the topic under
our consideration—the one on pictures, called "Lessons in
Looking," and another on recorded music, called "Music My
Rampart." For both there is a useful bibliography, and the
ways and means of starting a collection of the best pictures
and records.

Personally, I have used, with children from seven years
old or even younger, Geoffrey Holmes' *Children's Art Book,*
and later Anna Berry's *Art for Children* and *Pictures to Grow
Up With.* I have never used these formally, but have just
"left them around." You cannot force these things, and as
the children grow more interested they ask questions. When
the need for fine background material comes, V. M. Hillyer's
The Child's History of Art, at the time of writing out of print
but obtainable from the public libraries, is fun for family
reading. The Metropolitan Museum of Art, New York, and
the Museum of Fine Arts, Boston, kindly provided further
suggestions when I was looking for material for children.
Their lists are to be found in Chapter Ten. If, by the slow
accumulation of experience, we can train this generation to
perceive something of what the great artists are trying to express, we might have fewer people who go to art galleries with
an air of conscious virtue, and come home with nothing but
aching feet. Moreover, every child should eventually have a
good course in the history of art, to give reinforcement and
perspective to his earlier interest.[1]

Others are better qualified than I to give suggestions on
the teaching of drawing and painting: the parents usually hand

[1] For other suggestions on Art books for children see page 179.

over this task to the experts, and we can only trust to their guidance. Margaret Mead, the anthropologist, has an interesting point of view in her book, *And Keep Your Powder Dry:*

"Our art schools have sometimes enshrined tradition and taught the child to draw from casts and models of the studios, to imitate the Old Masters' line. But that line remains to him dead in all its loveliness because it has no relation to his immediacy of feeling, because if the child learns to love it he himself will die to all that moves the men around him and wander for ever among lost ghosts. That is one way. Other schools have left the children free, given them great lush brushes packed with raw color, given them pots of paint and let them use their sensitive enquiring fingers to map out the dimensions of their hearts, on very large sheets of paper. They have given them no tradition, no pattern, no single constricting instruction. What do we find? From the little child on whom the tradition of his society still rests lightly, beneath which his own peculiar undisciplined rhythms still thump with recognizable vigor —we get again lovely lines. But then as the shades of the prison house begin to close about the growing boy—and close they will as far as his own spontaneity is concerned, he learns to substitute a posture and a gesture which nine times out of ten would not have been his by choice—he loses this communication with his own heart, and there is nothing left . . . Freedom is not enough. Freedom that is its own goal has no design, but is only an impulse." [2]

We must be prepared for many revelations as we look at children's drawings. One kindergarten teacher sat back with a feeling of having told the story of the Flight into Egypt rather well and the children were absorbed in making drawings of the journey of the Holy Family. When they had fin-

[2] William Morrow & Co. Copyright 1942 by Margaret Mead. By permission.

ished, they brought them to her. One little boy displayed his picture with especial pride. The teacher looked—"Yes, I see Mary, and Joseph, and the baby," she said, "but what is that dark spot in the corner?" "You said they had to flee into Egypt," said the child, "that is the flea."

The term "visual education" is now part of the current scholastic vocabulary, and in religious education it means, I suppose, making the right pictures available to the pupils, and also the use of slides and movies in class instruction. In this region there are very great possibilities, for many children can be best approached and enlightened through the eye; we have seen how the promoters (of less worthy influence) of commercial propaganda have seized upon this truth. Most religious centers—councils of churches, and so on—have started libraries of the best films available, and collections of slides which can be borrowed for a small sum by the churches. The slides are excellent for helping in the appreciation of great pictures and for the teaching of Bible customs, geography, and church history. Children enjoy the moving pictures of Bible stories—e.g. The Cathedral Films [3]—in proportion to the amount of critical faculty they have developed. Almost all are helped by the faithful portrayal of the life in Bible times. I have talked with many children of various ages about these movies. To some they have been a genuine religious experience, as though the stirring of imagination satisfied a need and helped their growth. Most preferred the ones that do not show the face of Jesus—they like the restraint shown in portraying only His distant figure, but the younger ones will say, "*Why* couldn't we see Jesus' face? I want to see His face!" This attitude is due, I think, to the fact that, for the time being, they are living the movie and are not conscious of it

[3] 2921 West Alameda Ave., Burbank, Calif.

as something acted for them. Boys of about twelve, mostly from educated homes, revealed a whole range of opinions in a test we gave them after one of these movies was shown. These comments ranged from repulsion to enthusiasm. One gave the most elaborate instructions for technical improvements, after the manner of the scientifically-minded generation, as to the kind of lighting to be used to get a better impression of sunshine in the desert. One boy tried to tell in his limited, slightly embarrassed way, that it was terrible to try to depict what is too wonderful to be shown. He felt the whole show was sacrilege. I believe that these films, used for both adults and children, do a lot of good and very little harm: those who feel as this boy did, should not be expected to attend.

"Music," wrote a soldier on active service who was planning the future of his children, in a letter to his home, "is as natural as breathing to most children, and appealing through its natural rhythm and spiritual joy to their hearts, resolves many discords in their lives." We are seeking to strengthen the child's religious life by every worthy avenue of the spirit. Music is one of them.

We may count among the greatly blessed those fortunate children who, from the cradle, hear something other than popular music. They are fewer than we think, although a surprising number survive to become fine appreciators of both great music and swing music. The ideal is for the family to make music together, and for the child to have from the beginning simple songs and hymns as part of the pattern of everyday life. Certainly it should be part of the hour when children and parents can be together. If we cannot play, we can use some of the fine recordings available. In addition to this there is the obvious desirability of giving every child some instrument to play—he should have the chance to be well-taught. Perhaps there are more second- and third-rate teachers of music than of any other subject, and it is better not to be subjected to these and to have the edge of real musical perception dulled, than it is to remain in ignorance of the technique of playing an instrument. Training in the art of listening is every child's birthright, whether he performs or not. Schools in this country have made headway in musical appreciation.

In church schools religious music for children has remained at a low level. So many superintendents are, as with pictures, content with the weak and sentimental hymns. Publishers in the past few years have brought out a number of atrociously poor hymn books, with vividly colored illustrations of cherub-faced children; the hymns themselves are badly chosen and the harmonization is weak. Most church hymnals have ample good material. Christmas music is a perfect treasure trove of fine things, and we have elsewhere commented on the religious opportunities of these festive times. The significance of Christmas and Easter is written indelibly on the hearts and minds of those who can live through these various channels of expression. To the older child, perhaps in his early adolescence, Bach's *St. Matthew Passion* can come as a great revelation. Our children will hear plenty of poor music, and it is our bounden duty to see that what we offer in connection with their religious teaching should be of the highest calibre. Music can indeed give wings to the mind, and how near to a religious experience is the growth that comes through hearing great music we cannot measure; certainly it enlarges our life, lifts us nearer the place where the spirit rises up towards its Creator.

The following simple service, intended to last half an hour, was used for children between the ages of nine and eleven years. Its success depends upon preparation beforehand, which may have gone on for at least three Sundays previous.

The poem was chosen, not for its high literary value, but because it clothes a profound idea in rhythmic language understandable to the child, and to help knit together the theme of the whole service. Words like "penitent" and "trespasses" will have been explained beforehand: with children it is better to take nothing for granted, and the point of an entire service can be lost through misunderstanding one word.

A SERVICE OF WORSHIP
Used in a Junior Church for Grades IV–VI

THEME: FORGIVENESS.

Organ Prelude   *Soeur Monique*   Couperin

Processional Hymn "Savior teach me day by day"

Minister: God is a Spirit: they that worship Him must worship Him in Spirit and in Truth.

Children: God is Light: and if we walk in the light, as He is in the light, we have fellowship one with another.

Minister: God is love: and everyone that loveth is born of God and knoweth God.

Let us pray.

Minister and Children:

Teach me my God and King,
In all things Thee to see,
And what I do in anything
To do it as for Thee

Minister: (Collect for Quinquagesima)

"O Lord, who has taught us that all our doings without charity are nothing worth; send Thy Holy Ghost, and pour into our hearts that most excellent gift of charity, the very bond of peace and of all virtues, without which whosoever liveth is counted dead before thee.

162

> Grant this for thine only Son Jesus Christ's sake." Amen.

All: Lord of the loving heart
             May mine be loving too.
             Lord of the gentle hands,
             May mine be gentle too.
             Lord of the willing feet,
             May mine be willing too.
             So may I grow more like to Thee
             In all I say or do.

Psalm 32 (Blessed is he whose unrighteousness is forgiven)
The Lesson: Luke 15:3–10
             Colossians 3:12–19

Hymn: "In Heavenly Love Abiding"
             (Use the tune of Bach's *Passion Chorale* from
             the *Concord Song Book,* Grades IV–VI)

Short Sermon: Re-read this verse from Colossians 3, already
             read in the lesson. "Forbearing one another
             and forgiving one another, if any man have a
             quarrel against any: even as Christ forgave
             you, so also do ye."

This immense theme could well have a whole series of services devoted to it. I think it should try to show simply the likeness between the experience of being forgiven by God ("forgive us our trespasses") and the need for us to forgive other people ("as we forgive them that trespass against us"). Refer to the story of two lost things, the lost sheep and the lost piece of silver (they should know these stories well) and speak of the rejoicing when they were found. Jesus told these stories to show what God is like, and how He wants us to come to Him when we are truly sorry for what we have done wrong. Being sorry isn't enough, is it? Why?

If God is ready to forgive us, we also must learn to forgive.

Let us think about the way we say this every day in the Lord's Prayer. Is it easy to forgive people? It is very easy to see their faults. Being angry with people seems to shut us away from God for a time. Once a poet tried to tell us how she felt about this: she said

> I came into the quiet fields
>   With anger in my heart,
> And the fields sighed and said to me—
>   'With us thou hast no part.'
>
> 'No sweet communion canst thou know,
>   No peace nor beauty find
> While thou dost bear within thy breast
>   Evil against thy kind.'
>
> Sudden there sang a little bird,
>   His notes like silver rain
> Washed all my bitter wrath away
>   And I was clean again.[4]

Don't you think hearing the bird reminded the poet of God's love, and suddenly she felt sorry and made up her mind to try hard not to get so angry again? Then happiness came back.

Let us pray. We will say together the prayer Jesus taught us, and we shall know again how He felt about forgiving people who are mean to us:

All: The Lord's Prayer.
All: Still kneeling, sing:

[4] Teresa Hooley, "Absolution" from *Selected Poems of Teresa Hooley*, Jonathan Cape, Ltd.

Choral Response:
> God be in my head
> And in my understanding.
> God be in my mouth
> And in my speaking;
> God be in my heart
> And in my thinking:
> God be at mine end
> And at my departing.

Recessional Hymn "He who would valiant be."
The Minister "Grant O Lord that when we leave Thy house
we may not leave Thy presence, but go with us wherever
we may go, unto our life's end."
Organ Postlude: "All Glory be to God on High" Bach

We have referred elsewhere to the nomenclature of hymns,
and its influence upon the child's idea of God. I have always
felt that much harm is done by lines like

> There's a friend for little children,
> Above the bright blue sky.

We have seen that the little child instinctively feels the
"nearness" of God and why do we push Him away? Other
hymns made God into a stranger sitting on a throne, being
ministered to by obliging cherubs. The anthropomorphic
idea of God is natural at the beginning, but we must not
relegate Him to the far distant ether. I remember, too, a
little boy asking repeatedly for the hymn "about the boy
who stole the watch." We puzzled for a long time, and finally
discovered that he wanted the hymn telling about Samuel,

called "Hush'd was the evening hymn," and the line he misunderstood was "His watch the little Levi kept." Attend any practice for the Junior Choirs which fortunately exist in many churches, and by questioning find out if they understand much of what they are singing. However, these choirs are a fine opportunity to make a contribution to the religious education of the children who take part in them. All children love pageantry, and we must try to make the experience of singing in Church something more than the pleasure of coming in, usually in some form of vestment, and having Aunt Mary in the congregation say how cunning you looked sitting up there. Junior Choirs usually begin to take children at an age when they are ready to *contribute* something to the service, and you are offering them the valuable experience of giving. If the person training the singers is not qualified to understand their religious perplexities, team work is good, and it is possible to combine musical and religious instruction to a valuable degree.

Without vision, we are told, the people perish. Poetry is vision, and is more desperately needed today than at any time in the history of mankind. I want to show how this belief is supported by three great thinkers of our time. First, Evelyn Underhill, in a lecture to teachers, said:

"Poetry is the great revealer of reality, a great incentive to worship; for it nourishes the sense of wonder, *perpetually breaks through the hard crust of practical life,* and lets in the other-worldly light. I am sure that the side of religion which most closely approaches poetry, which cannot be expressed at all without the use of poetry, is of the greatest importance to the Christian educationalist, and especially perhaps at the present time; for the utilitarian spirit, which has gained such a dreadful ascendancy in modern education, has even infected much modern religion." [5]

Then we hear W. MacNeile Dixon, in his brilliant survey of modern thought, given in the Gifford Lectures after a long analysis covering more than four hundred pages, dissecting the findings of science and philosophy—say:

"To believe life an irremediable disaster, the heavens and earth an imbecility, is to my way of thinking hard indeed. Since I am not prepared to believe this world a misery-go-round, a torture chamber, a furnace of senseless affliction; since I am not prepared to believe the fiery, invincible soul a by-blow, a lamentable accident; I prefer to put my trust in the larger vision of the poets. To fortify our minds it is to them we have to return, and yet again return. They alone have understood. 'It exceeds all imagination to conceive,' wrote Shelley, 'what would have been the moral condition of our world if the poets had never been born! . . . And it is to their inextinguishable sympathy with humanity that they owe their understanding. Not to science or philosophy, but to their profounder appreciation of the strange situation in which we find ourselves, to their sense of the pitiful estate of man, who, with all the forces of nature proclaiming an alien creed, still holds to its intuitions . . . to his passion for justice, his trust in the affections of his heart, his love of the lovely, his lonely struggle for the best, however clumsy and mistaken he may be in his present estimates of what is indeed best . . . It is in the exalted thoughts and still more soaring dreams of 'that wild swan the soul,' the admirable lunacies, the sudden gleams that illuminate the sombre landscape of human life that the poets find the revelation of the vital truth." [6]

[5] *Collected Papers*, p. 234, Longmans.
[6] *The Human Situation*, p. 436, Longmans, Green & Co. By permission.

Children and Religion

Finally, Sir Richard Livingstone in his remarkable book, *On Education:*

> "Most people are shortsighted; the poet has long sight, and, where others see nothing or vague uncertain shapes, he sees life with vivid colors and sharp outlines, and enables us to see it too. That is the deepest value of poetry. We may enjoy the music or its richness of language; but its essential virtue is its revealing power. Without poetry we are more than half blind. . . . Literature is desirable—to enlarge experience. It is necessary to interpret it; to do what few, if any, can do unaided by themselves—penetrate below the surface of phenomena to their inner and real meaning. Poetry, supposed to be 'highbrow' and remote, deals for the most part with the world of everyday. Its subjects are ordinary things seen by people who are not ordinary . . . the mark of a poet is that he interprets life more generally, more disinterestedly, more for itself and in itself, more in its permanent, and less in its fleeting aspects than other men. Human progress depends chiefly on what men see in life, and how they interpret it; and the ages in which the world has moved forward are those rare ages when men of religious or poetic or intellectual levels have caught sight of levels higher than those in which the world is moving. . . . Poetry, with religion to which it is closely allied, is the great source of the phenomena among which we live." [7]

In this book, Sir Richard also points out that fifty years ago, "nearly everyone through readings from the Bible, in prayers, and sometimes in sermons heard once a week a great philosophy of life expounded. Much of the seed fell on stony places," he says, "yet whatever the defects of ministers and congregations, it was something to have listened, even with

[7] *On Education*, p. 82, Macmillan. Copyright 1944. By permission.

half-shut ears, to the sacred book of the purest and greatest of religions, and the hearers learnt, if not to speak, at least to understand, a common language in thought and conduct. *The loss might not be so serious if some even partly adequate substitute had taken its place."* He points out that we are worse off for guidance than the Graeco-Roman world, which had its great popular philosophies. These, he says, "were thrown out of work by Christianity, and we have no sort of substitute for religion. Modern philosophy, in so far as it is more than a technique of thought, is only available to the tiny class that understands its language. What are our equivalents for the church-going of our fathers, or the philosophies of the ancient world? What are today the chief constant influences on the minds of the masses of the people? They are the film and the cheap press, uttering loudly and with the confusion of many inharmonious voices such doctrines as the prospect of immediate profit inspires. . . . I do not believe," he concludes "that our need can be fully met except through religion," but he does suggest that "education based on, or largely infused with, history and literature rightly taught might help to bring some order into the spiritual chaos of today." [8]

The standard of poetry offered to most of our children in the lower grades of the present-day schools will certainly not prepare them to appreciate the work of the great poets when they are older. I like the old-fashioned custom of calling verses churned out by all and sundry—"verses"; and if ever they managed to achieve the greater merit and perform some of the functions just mentioned, we can then raise them to the exalted name of "poetry." What is so frequently published and taught to children, especially to little children, is sentimental in the extreme, or just foolishly empty. The religious

[8] *Ibid.,* p. 85.

jingles of the primary department of many church schools are very poor indeed; by the fourth grade the intelligent child will begin to parody them, and the seeds of despising religious instruction are sown. Too often teachers think that any pretty verses will do for the young. One desperate professor likens those who write such drivel to penny-in-the-slot machines. "Let nature drop in a sunset," says he, "or life a heart throb, there is a little click and a poem drops warm and soft into your outstretched hand. The austere requirement of clarity and imagery, of precision and lucidity of thought, of compression and balanced harmony, of form—these troubled the sentimentalist not a whit. All that is necessary is to reach out into an atmosphere of rosy mist, and capture the first nebulous notion that floats into one's grasp . . . The sentimentalist escapes the stern travail of thought."

Parents must once again come to the rescue. Every household with children in it, should have some good anthologies for children, beginning with Mother Goose. Read, in Paul Hazard's delightful book, *Books, Children, and Men,* his exquisite essay on nursery rhymes, and you will have a new feeling about these traditional, childish songs, which are "often only music, singing vowels, repetitions of sound, simple cadences stressed, full and sonorous rhymes. They are not unconscious of the fact that by placing rhythm at the beginning of life they are conforming to the general order of the universe. They have a harmony all their own that is strange, mocking, and tender. The sense is of less importance than the sound."

Some of the books of poetry my own children happen to have grown up on are the following:

The Real Mother Goose (Junior Edition), published by Rand McNally
The Child's Garden of Verses, ROBERT LOUIS STEVENSON

The Golden Staircase, compiled by Louis Chisholm (Nelson)
> An excellent collection for all ages, containing some fine religious verse as well as others.
> Another perhaps even finer collection:

Bells Across the Sand, compiled by Annis Duff and Gladys Adshead (Houghton-Mifflin). *Excellent* for all ages.

This Singing World, compiled by Louis Untermeyer (Harcourt Brace)

Come Hither, compiled by Walter de la Mare (Knopf)

Bells and Grass, by Walter de la Mare (Viking)

Silver Pennies, compiled by B. J. Thompson (Macmillan)

More Silver Pennies (Macmillan)

Nonsense Songs and Stories, by Edward Lear (Warne)

And of course the books of A. A. Milne.

Mrs. Duff, in the book *Bequest of Wings,* previously suggested for parental reading, gives a longer list in her bibliography, and has written two brief but pleasant chapters, *Poetry in the Nursery* and *Poetry for Children.*

Of course, children vary very much in their response to words, but we should give every child a chance, and when the subject of the poem interests him, even if he is not at first sensitive to the rhythm and cadence (which is the more usual beginning) he may begin to manifest interest. You can see tense little faces, at home and away from home, relax, and the bright light of imagination, which lies behind all the real activities of mind and action, begin to light up their faces. And please do not forget some good nonsense; to the end of my days I shall be pondering on the "why" of this elusive light in the human mind: we can only know that it gives perspective and sanity to the whole gamut of human experience, and by some small miracle makes us more ready for deeper reality.

But above all, we have the poetry of the Bible. The book

of Psalms is the greatest collection of religious poetry in the world. If carefully chosen, and especially if read aloud, children respond to its beauty; in time they also appreciate its wisdom:

> The heavens declare the glory of God;
> And the firmament sheweth his handywork.
> Day unto day uttereth speech,
> And night unto night sheweth knowledge.
> There is no speech nor language,
> Where their voice is not heard. (Psalm 19)

> Bless the Lord, O my soul.
> O Lord my God, thou art very great;
> Thou art clothed with honour and majesty.
> Who coverest thyself with light as with a garment:
> Who stretchest out the heavens like a curtain:
> Who layeth the beams of his chambers in the waters:
> Who maketh the clouds his chariot:
> Who walketh upon the wings of the wind. . . .
> Man goeth forth unto his work
> And to his labour until the evening.
> O Lord, how manifold are thy works!
> In wisdom hast thou made them all:
> The earth is full of thy riches. . . .

Psalm 104, from which this last passage was taken, is a suitable one to use for choric speaking. Many passages from the Bible can be used thus, and this is an excellent way for a whole group of children to become familiar with some of the finest chapters in the King James Version.

Evelyn Underhill, in her classic, *Worship,* points out that "Even the great liturgic value of the psalter does not entirely depend on the spiritual truths which the psalmists con-

vey: but at least to some extention that peculiar quality in
poetry, which tends to arouse and liberate the transcendental
sense."

The Book of Job is full of poetic material, typified by the
triumphant climax in the last chapter:

> I know that thou canst do every thing,
> And that no thought can be withholden from thee.
> Who is he that hideth counsel without knowledge?
> Therefore have I uttered that I understood not;
> Things too wonderful for me, which I knew not.
> Hear I beseech thee, and I will speak:
> I will demand of thee, and declare thou unto me.
> I have heard of thee by the hearing of the ear:
> But now mine eye seeth thee.

(The book of Job would obviously be read with much older
children than the Psalms, and then not without considerable
study on the part of the adults, in perhaps one of the books
suggested in the previous chapter.)

For those who have not heard the Bible as little children,
and even to some to whom we have thought it familiar, there
comes at times a sudden revelation of its beauty. I remember
reading to a twelve-year-old, brought up in a Christian home,
David's lament for Saul and Jonathan:

> The beauty of Israel is slain upon thy high places:
> How are the mighty fallen!
> Tell it not in Gath,
> Publish it not in the streets of Askelon;
> Lest the daughters of the Philistines rejoice,
> Lest the daughters of the uncircumcised triumph.
> Ye mountains of Gilboa, let there be no dew,
> Neither let there be rain, upon you, nor fields of offerings:

For there the shield of the mighty is vilely cast away,
The shield of Saul, as though he had not been anointed
    with oil. . . .
Saul and Jonathan were lovely and pleasant in their lives,
And in their death they were not divided:
They were swifter than eagles,
They were stronger than lions. . . .
How are the mighty fallen in the midst of the battle!
O Jonathan, thou wast slain in thine high places,
I am distressed for thee, my brother Jonathan:
Very pleasant hast thou been unto me:
Thy love to me was wonderful,
Passing the love of women.
How are the mighty fallen,
And the weapons of war perished!

(II Samuel, 1).

The child was in bed, and an astonished voice came from among the pillows, "Is that the Bible? I didn't think there was anything as lovely as that in it!"

Isaiah is full of riches, and the New Testament will yield an endless store of poetry, besides the more usual ones like the Beatitudes (Mt. 5:1–12; Lk. 6:20–26) and Paul's sermon on Charity (I Cor., 13). *The Book of Books* (selections from the King James Version), mentioned in the last chapter has some fine chapters of Biblical poetry.

"If Jesus is to become real to the students," said Dr. Adelaide Case in an article on "Creative Education for Adults," "the students must themselves make him so." She cites the usual methods of teaching the New Testament, all of which are valuable, and then says, "They do not do enough. It is possible to pass through them all and at the same time to miss the vital reality of the life of Jesus. To make anything real our imagination must play upon it. We must dramatize it for ourselves

in our own thought-life, mix it with the stuff of our emotional world, re-create it with the essential fabric of our lives.
. . . Their attitude toward the gospel records must be primarily critical (in the best sense of that word) and creative."

It may be helpful to notice a child's attempt to express her
religious ideas in words.

In a garden in Europe, when the threat of the Second World
War was so dark that grown-up fears had penetrated into the
atmosphere of children's lives, I heard a six-year-old singing
a song she made up as she went along:

> The birds may be His army
> And the flowers may be His cloak.

At eight years old she wrote a Christmas carol:

MARY'S SONG

> The little Jesus
> Came to me
> I laid Him down
> Upon my knee.
> Sleep, little Jesus,
> Hush, hush.
> In a manger
> Out of danger
> There he was laid,
> Lovely babe.
> Rest, rest
> In your warm nest!
> Rest! [9]

[9] "Mary's Song," Horn Book, Inc.

175

By eleven she was trying her hand at plays, one of which was called *The Wooing of Mary*, A Drama in Three Acts, a mixture of immaturity, perception, and semi-medieval background, the last brief scene was a celebration of the betrothal, and ended:

FRIEND. Come, good friends, and break bread and drink wine with us.

MARY. (To Joseph) Let us stay out here a few minutes.

JOSEPH. Yea. (Others go out) I have a gift for thee, Mary. (He brings from the fold of his robe a tiny lamb.) Symbol of a son.

MARY. I know my task.

JOSEPH. And I.

MARY. Glory to Jehovah in the highest and on earth peace.

JOSEPH. For ever more.

CURTAIN

At twelve years there is the pre-adolescent's especial delight in nature:

MID-WINTER

Wind, stay your taunting blows,
Trees, bend low beneath your icy grasp,
Squirrels, hunched and cold,
Dare not stir from bleak hollow.

From the steel gray sky,
Burst forth a rosy light.
The river has cast off his icy cloak,
And leaps in triumph.

Ah wind, be lulled and still,
The Christ Child comes.

A year later there are the signs of the adolescent desire to "find oneself."

THOUGHTS

As morning slowly wakens,
My thoughts soar to God;
Gladness and sorrow together
Are twin larks ascending.

Musings of gay and great things,
Cruel and sad,
Contrast of dark and light
Are now winging upward.

Thoughts of pride and resentment,
Gratefulness and remorse,
Many conflicting passions
Rise into space.

Wishes slight as a sparrow's chirping,
Thoughts longing and prayerful,
Empty or brightly hopeful,
Fleeing to God.

By fourteen, a deeper conception of the prophets was coming, and a sense of world tragedy.

HOSEA

He shared with Christ
The pain and glory
Of supreme loneliness.
No man knew him;

Only his tiny sons and God
Could sense such tenderness.

He wept solitary tears
And pleaded:
"O Ephraim, repent
And turn from sin.
The Assyrian lion crouches;
He will spring.
There is time to live as brothers,
Before the day of Yahweh
Vanishes.

He wed Gomer.
Shiftlessly she flung
Away his pardoning love.
So Israel,
Blindly wicked, hurled back to God
Compassion from above.[10]

Parents interested to see some of the fine products of children's imagination—painting, verse, songs, plays, etc.—should borrow from a library *Creative Expression: The Development of Children in Art, Music, Literature or Dramatics,* edited by Gertrude Hartman and Ann Shumaker.

Encourage the children to make their own Bible plays, as well as to act out those written for them. *Ventures in Dramatics,* by Hulda Niebuhr, is very helpful. It gives an account of dramatics with church school pupils aged ten to fifteen years, and shows how a play can be part of a worship service. An interesting example in this book is the dramatization of some events in the life of William Tyndale, to whom we

[10] Editor's note: the poem on this page and those immediately preceding were written by the author's daughter, Ann P. Chaplin.

referred in the previous chapter. I am sure that children, having studied books on the making of our Bible, and then trying to live in imagination in those times and present their discoveries to others in dramatic form, make those events part of their inspiration for life.

CREATIVE ACTIVITIES AND DRAMATICS

KELLEY, M. and ROURKES, N., *Let's Make a Mural,* Fearon Publishers, 2263 Union Street, San Francisco, California

ALLSTROM, E., *Let's Play a Story,* Friendship Press

SIKS, GERALDINE B., *Creative Dramatics, An Art for Children,* Harper

KEISER, ARMILDA, *Here's How and When,* Friendship Press

LOBINGIER, ELIZABETH M., *Activities in Child Education,* Pilgrim Press (Bibliography) *Plays for the Church* (National Council of Churches)

SUGGESTIONS ON ART BOOKS FOR CHILDREN
(Obtainable from Libraries)

Stories of the Italian Artists, edited by ELIZABETH SEELEY
    These are adaptations and translations of selected passages from the great Italian book by Vasari. Here the child will read a more biographical approach.

A Picture Book of British Art, E. M. O'R. DICKEY

Guide to the Paintings in the National Gallery, London, C. J. HOLMES. A Curator of Paintings says this is excellent and entirely within the range of an intelligent eleven year old. It is full of pictures and comments on them.

How to Study Pictures, CHARLES T. COFFIN, is another book that has been suggested.

Children and Religion

The Metropolitan Museum in New York has an excellent series of "Picture Books" covering various fields of interest. There is no one book on European painting. The book *Dutch Paintings* contains excellent black and white reproductions. The introduction, however, is definitely for adults. *50 Great Paintings* has no text but large black and white reproductions of famous paintings in the Museum. The most suitable for our purpose would be "Winslow Homer," which gives an account of the artist's life and contains reproductions in black and white of his paintings in the Metropolitan Museum.

What and What Not, KAY PARKER. A brief introduction to architecture, sculpture and painting in picture book form.

Treasure Trails in Art, ANNA CURTIS CHANDLER. An excellent introduction to twenty European artists. Each story tells about an artist and a specific picture he painted.

Story Lives of Master Artists, Series 1 and 2 by ANNA CURTIS CHANDLER.

Art in the New Land, CHARLIE MAY SIMON. Dutton. Well-written biographical accounts of famous American artists beginning with Colonial times.

N.B.

See also a very interesting presentation called "The Arts as a Media for Participation," in *The Dynamics of Christian Education,* by IRIS V. CULLY (Westminster 1958) pages 136–142.

Also MENDELOWITZ, D. *Children are Artists* (Stanford Un. Press 1953).

I should like to turn for a few moments to a position in secular education parallel to the one we have been considering in religious education, although we are agreed that we cannot separate the two. A Red Cross worker in the Second World War, whose duty it was to supply "doughnuts, coffee and conversation" to a minimum of 6000 men a week overseas, and who estimates that in her 132 weeks of service she talked—and listened—to thousands of them, set forth her findings in an article called "They was Robbed," which was published in *The Brearley Bulletin* and parts of which we reproduce with the permission of the author, Miss Lydia Sherwood.

"We consider it a tremendous privilege," she says, "to have known as many of them as we did. . . . They were, quite simply, wonderful. They were funny, scared, brave, bored, gay, perceptive, and resourceful. They had humor and dignity. They had ingenuity and 'know-how' unequalled by any army and constituting one of the great strengths of our own. They had everything—except an education; or any of the equipment for living that education is supposed to give.

"Based on my observations overseas, the principal failures of the American public school system may be listed as follows:

"1. It has failed to give its students a frame of reference into which they can fit ideas, facts, and experiences not previously encountered.

"2. It has dulled, rather than sharpened, their intellectual curiosity and desire to learn—causing them to reject, rather than to welcome, new ideas and experiences.

"3. It has left them (to use Charles G. Bolte's term) 'Politically illiterate.'

"4. It has failed to provide them with any set of moral or ethical values to counterbalance the false set of values offered by the movies, the radio, and the advertisements . . .

"First, to explain what I mean by 'a frame of reference.' It was almost impossible to realize how little the G. I.'s knew about even the most familiar aspects of history, art, literature, or languages—how fantastically innocent they were of the cultural heritage with which we assumed that everybody had at least a nodding acquaintance. For example, they would gladly walk with a Red Cross girl to the ruins of Tiberius' palace at Capri, and a delightful walk would be had by all. But it was hard at first to enthrall them with any accounts of the eccentric Emperor, or the palace itself, or the life that went on there, since they had never heard of the Roman Empire. . . . They had never heard of Michelangelo or Leonardo da Vinci, of Donatello or Titian, of Galileo or Dante; nor were Shelley, Byron, or the Brownings, whose paths we also crossed, more familiar to them. They had never heard of Hannibal (another old Italian campaigner), or of *The Merchant of Venice,* or of the Renaissance. They had no historical perspective to make their discomforts more bearable. . . .

"I am not saying that I advocate a morbid preoccupation with the past. But a world in which the past simply does not exist seems to me appallingly flat, grey, and one-dimensional. It seemed especially so overseas, where the present was dreary and dangerous and the future hypothetical. To sum up—it seemed bitterly ironical that men should be asked to suffer and die for Western civilization, without having previously been told what Western civilization was."

The writer goes on to expound her ideas about these conditions, and finally comes to the part that concerns us most and comes nearest to what we are trying to build in the children we teach; she comes to the question of moral and ethical values. "Many boys I knew (fundamentally kind, decent boys) seemed to have no personal code of morals or ethics, no behavior pattern except what had been imposed by the American society in which they grew up. Overseas, they were not only uprooted from that society, but exposed to almost irresistible temptations. . . . But you cannot censure the black-marketing or looting G. I. without also censuring the system which sent him out with no clear idea of right and wrong *as such;* and with an ingrained conviction that money and possession, however acquired, spell success.

"That there is nothing wrong with their basic qualities of heart and spirit is proved by the gallantry with which they fought, and the fortitude with which they endured the months and years of suffering. They had no political or ideological conviction to fight for; no feeling that they were defending the right against the powers of darkness . . . they fought simply for each other—because the lives of a whole squad depended on each man in it. When men can show such magnificent qualities of loyalty and devotion to their own countrymen, it should not be too difficult to transfer the allegiance to a larger fellowship—the human race."

The suggested remedies are as follows, and it is interesting to compare them with what we have tried to outline as the fundamental requirements in religious education:

"1. Short courses, at least, in *each* of the following: Ancient History, Mediaeval History, English History, Modern European History. At least two years of English Literature, and at least one of History of Art. This much, it seems to me, must be regarded as the birthright of every citizen of the Western World.

"2. Compulsory study of at least one foreign language; accompanied, if possible, with some study of the history, customs, and cultures, of the country selected.

"3. A course outlining at least the underlying composition of each of the following forms of government: Democracy, Totalitarianism, Socialism, and Communism. What are they? What are the basic differences between them? How many of the liberties we now enjoy do we owe to the ancient Greeks; how many to the long struggle of the British for civil rights?

"4. A course, or series of courses, giving—without bias towards any religious sect or creed—some idea of the trend of man's thought on moral and spiritual questions throughout the ages, emphasizing the basic theme of man's responsibility to society and to his own best self which appears in all religions."

You will remember that others have concluded that, while the spiritual chaos of today might be in some measure dispelled by history and literature rightly taught, the need can be fully met by only one thing—religion. All the remedies suggested above would help to enrich the conception, and give perspective to the whole life. Lewis Mumford, in his *Condition of Man* gives the verdict: "Religion, art, ethics, philosophy, poetry, science—these are the ultimate agents in man's self-transformation. All man's other acts, deeds, acquisitions, discoveries, are significant only to the extent that they finally find expression in these realms."

In observing the need for transcendence in our present world, we turn to the remedy offered by the uplifting power of great art. Allied to the basis of sound religious growth, I believe that the arts are invaluable in helping to develop a comprehension of God. Every child responds to the beauty of pictures, or poetry, of great literature, and music, he transcends himself and reaches out—"going beyond." These things go further than anything he can say himself, and stand by him all his days. In a report made by Quaker day schools, qualities enumerated as having been inspired by the arts are "awe, wonder, love, exultation, enthusiasm." Are not all these needed in developing a religiously-inclined life, especially in the growing ability to worship?

I believe that in the education of children art can be a bridge between them and God—not a substitute for prayer, but closely allied to it. Art is the expression of the living spirit in our lives, showing men to themselves while, consciously or unconsciously, the artist gives back to the world what he has discovered of God. The enlargement of the spirit, a release, as it were, into greater dimensions, which is made possible by great art, makes a fuller conception of God possible. Without it, we lose our vision, we become "bound to the sphere of the biological and material," and thus restrict the free creativity of the soul: our horizon shrinks. Perhaps the experience of listening to great music is an example of this stretching out of the soul.

Do you mean, you may say, pointing to Brother Lawrence busy in his kitchen, that you can practice the presence of God only if you have a developed artistic taste? By no means. The religious life is in itself an art, a creative ability. We are considering ways of enriching this life.

Beyond all this, and the plane to which all artistic experience should take us, lies the need for God in a more organized religious life, for many to be found in the Christian Church.

The great mission of American education, says Professor Robert Ulich in *The Fundamentals of Democratic Education* is "to guide humanity towards the *enduring* sources of regeneration." He says elsewhere that "the immediate goal must be to instil into general education a spirit that will open the way for a religious outlook upon the universe." Professor Ulich contends that the modern capacity for faith has decreased, and that we feel uneasy and uncertain if we go beyond the realm of "experimentally and scientifically proven ideas into the realm of the supernatural." If we could raise the standard of our teaching in religious education, so that its quality might equal the best in secular education, we should be doing vital work. It would ultimately permeate the field of state education, and there would not be so great a gulf.

Religion in every age and civilization is striving to be renewed, and it needs every worthy avenue of man's thought through which to achieve that renewal. Why, when our children ask for bread, do we give them a stone?

CHAPTER TEN

Ways of Approach

III. THROUGH BOOKS

"I like books that remain faithful to the very essence of art; namely, those that offer to children an intuitive and direct way of knowledge, a simple beauty capable of being perceived immediately, arousing in their souls a vibration which will endure all their lives. . . . And books that awaken in them, not maudlin sentimentality, but sensibility; that enable them to share in great human emotions; that give them respect for universal life—that of animals, of plants; that teach them not to despise everything that is mysterious in creation and in man. . . . I like books of knowledge; not those that want to encroach upon recreation, upon leisure, pretending to be able to teach anything without drudgery. There is no truth in that . . . I like them especially when they distill from all the different kinds of knowledge the most difficult and the most necessary—that of the human heart . . .

"I know very well that these conditions are difficult to fulfil . . . They are even more imperative than when it is a question of a good book for men, which in itself is not so easy to produce. But to misshape young souls, to profit by a certain facility that one may possess to add to the number of indigestible and sham books. . . . that is what I call oppressing children."

—PAUL HAZARD
[in "Books, Children, and Men"]
Pub. by Horn Book, Inc. Tr. Marguerite Mitchell

Paul Hazard, whose words we have quoted at the head of this chapter, has written his "Books, Children and Men" in order to expound the fascinating thesis that the children's books in any one country are the measure of a nation's awareness of the rights of the individual! This delightful book, rather like a collection of essays, is a joy to read. Parents and teachers who are really desirous of finding the best books, may well be proud of what has been done in this country; I don't know whether with our appalling hoards of funny books we are guilty of producing some of the worst juvenile books in the world; but Paul Hazard ventures to think that we also produce the best. He is aware on the one hand of the invasion of machinery, and of the soul confused by material progress, of the evils of standardized recreation and movies for the only relaxation of many young minds. "But do not overlook," says he, "the facts that can be put just as fairly on the other side of the scales. And because it concerns us here, do not overlook the vigorous spirit that persists wherever the sympathetic question of childhood is brought up. What wonderful efforts have been made to safeguard it, to nourish its spirit, to provide the choicest foods for its curiosity! Explorers set forth from America to all the countries of the world to bring back new story material. Artists, designers, engravers, painters from all the countries in the world arrive in America, invited to decorate the pages of children's books. The élite of the country, that long-suffering élite which rebels against any diminution of the spirit, surrounds the coming generation with a solicitude probably unequaled anywhere as a treasury of hope." He thus makes the stocking of our national juvenile bookshelves sound like the building of the temple of Solomon.

Even allowing for the engaging eulogy of Paul Hazard's style, we can take heart when we borrow from the library such volumes as *Realms of Gold in Children's Books,* by Bertha E. Mahony and Elinor Whitney, and *My Roads,* by Anne Carroll Moore. The first of these gives you "the notice, and sometimes the analysis, of all the books in the English language, original or translated, that a child could wish for." The second discusses children's books, and teenage books, in relation to life, and gives lists of representative books published, both, of course, including many reprints of the classics.

The Horn Book published at 585 Boylston Street, Boston, Mass. has always represented fine standards in reviewing reading for children and young people.

With these standbys available, I think it is outside the purpose of this book to attempt to give further suggestions as to children's general reading. In this chapter, however, we hope that a few comments and lists on children's religious books today will be of practical use to parents.

We have come a long way in juvenile religious books since somebody wrote *Peep of Day,* the standard work for three generations in the last century, which could inform you, as Eleanor Acland tells us, "How the earth, sun, and stars had been created, how alone the soul of man can be delivered from sin and eternal death, with all the pat assurance of Mrs. Beeton giving a recipe for making plum-pudding. . . . We read them trustfully, Sunday after Sunday, and accepted them, as also those parts of the Bible that were read aloud or narrated to us, as statements of unquestionable fact." [1]

Many of the story books handed down to us have a distinct religious flavor—the heroine often died slowly of consumption and gave exhortations to piety before she left this world, having first converted the whole family. This was followed

[1] *Goodbye for the Present,* p. 155, Hodder & Stoughton.

by an era when the entire adult world was so busy dabbling in the higher criticism of the Bible, and later in science and psychology, that they were afraid to write religious books for children. We have seen how they were so confused themselves that they thought they had better let their children discover their own religion. We have seen the results of that, and how we are driven back to God in our own time. We have seen how the pendulum has swung and, while few people now believe that the Bible is the dictated word of God, it is recognized as the story of man's search for God: out of this belief, and backed by a deeper understanding of the needs of children, have come some of the fine religious books for children available today.

And what is wrong with the still greater number of poor religious books? They are so watered-down and sentimental that the healthy modern child thinks religion is a weak kind of fairy story, while pictures of an effeminate Jesus support the view. The story of man's search for religion is more thrilling than anything in the world—yet we offer them this "pink cloud stuff." Other authors, seeing this pitfall, set out to put everything on a platter, and when scanned by a true scholar, their books are found to be pseudo-scientific, and also not sound from the archeologist's point of view, which means that the child must eventually unlearn what he has read if he wants a sound basis for a lasting faith.

The books listed here are not suggested because they are necessarily representative of the heights of perfection, but because they are the best I have discovered at the time of writing. Some have already been referred to elsewhere in the book: for convenience sake I have re-listed them here. All have been tried out with individual children and with classes, but even this cannot, obviously, guarantee their being "just the right thing" for the individual child. Books for parents and teachers are obviously only a brief selection from the great number written about children.

As time goes on, I hope there will be more early books, especially first "readers" for children, in which life is sometimes portrayed as not going smoothly, books in which Mother is occasionally sick or tired, when plans go wrong, and life is not all fun. It helps to have the adults not always in a benevolent mood. The *Martin and Judy* books, three volumes by Verna Hills and Sophia Fahs are not entirely what I mean, but they give the everyday experiences of two children and a dog and dare to meet such eventualities as going to the hospital, and even a death in the family.

Books are not a substitute for life, or for religious experience. Knowing *about* Christianity is not the same as a living experience of it; but it is to be hoped that some of the following may open the doors that lead towards a clearer conception of God, or that they may at least prevent some of the worst stumbling blocks from falling across the little child's road to God.

BOOKS OF PRAYERS FOR LITTLE CHILDREN
FROM THREE YEARS OLD

1. *A Child's Grace,* HAROLD BURDEKIN, Dutton
   From about three years old, this book, illustrated by photographs of real children, is much loved. It helps the child to make his own prayers, for each picture illustrates a line of childish thanksgiving, and is related to daily experience.
2. *Prayer for Little Things,* ELEANOR FARJEON, Houghton Mifflin

3. *Prayer for a Child,* RACHEL FIELD, Macmillan
  We group these two together because they are both prayers about everyday things, beautifully illustrated by Elizabeth Orton Jones, and much loved by little children. We hope, since children have taken them so completely to their hearts, that they will always be used with readings from the King James Version, and with the great prayers and collects of the Christian tradition, not instead of these treasures.

4. *Thank You, God,* VIVYEN BREMNER, Macmillan

5. *Good and Gay,* MARY OSBORN. Imported, from Challenge, Ltd., London
  These little books are very helpful for home worship and teaching, for children aged three to six years, and six to eight years respectively. They contain poems, prayers, and charming pictures. They are especially useful as a bedtime resource, and have little lessons on the Christian seasons to add to their charm.

6. *Small Rain* (or another title by these authors) JESSIE and ELIZABETH ORTON JONES
  This is not a book of "regular prayers" but a little collection of well-chosen Bible passages illustrated with pictures of children. It is extremely popular with many families, and a good way for the little child to absorb parts of the Bible in a very suitable way —he naturally wants to have the text read. One small girl said, "The pictures don't say what the words say," which is a comment on our adult way of presenting things. Most children love this book, all the same.

A DEVOTIONAL BOOK FOR CHILDREN 8 YRS. AND OLDER

Youth Talks with God, AVERY BROOKE, Scribners
  A unique book of prayers for modern children. Everyday life and problems are brought to God.

Ways of Approach—Books

BIBLE STORIES

(See also Chapter Eight for suggested Children's Bibles in the King
James Version)

1. For little children, from three years old:
   Bible Books for Small People. NELSON
       This series of twelve little books, about the size of the *Peter
   Rabbit* volumes, and made in the same style, that is, having a
   few words on a page and a picture opposite, are very valuable to
   use with little children from three to four years old, and for a
   year or two after that. They ask for them many times and eventually know them by heart, after which they pretend to read
   them aloud. When they can read, we find them borrowing them
   with solemnity from the library. There are some New Testament
   ones, e.g. *When Jesus was a Boy,* and *Jesus, Friend of Little
   Children,* which are much loved. Then there are some Christmas
   ones, e.g. *The Song the Shepherds Heard;* some parables, the
   best of which is *The Shepherd and His Sheep;* and some Old
   Testament ones, e.g. *Baby Moses,* and *Isaac of the Tents.*

2. *Once There Was a Little Boy,* DOROTHY KUNHARDT, Viking (From
   five years old and up.)
       This is a quiet, enchanting story of Jesus' childhood, with ex-
   quisite illustrations.

3. *Joseph, Moses, Ruth, and David,* retold for little children by MAUD
   and MISKA PETERSHAM, Winston
       They can be had separately or bound together under the title,
   "Stories from the Old Testament." For little children.

4. *The Christ Child, as told by Matthew and Luke,* made by MAUD
   and MISKA PETERSHAM. Doubleday
       Although previously mentioned, no list is complete without this
   classic. It is fortunately now widely known and suitable at all
   times of the year.

5. *Joseph. The Story of Twelve Brothers*, FLORENCE KLABER, Beacon Press
    Children from about nine to twelve years old enjoy this.
6. *The Story of the Bible,* WALTER RUSSELL BOWIE, Abingdon
    This is the standard book for a continuous Bible narrative, and keeps close to the text of the King James Version. It emphasizes the search of man for God throughout the ages. Professor Bowie is a Biblical scholar of great standing, and has brought his extensive learning to bear upon this work, which should be in every family library. He has also done a "portrait" of Jesus, called *The Story of Jesus,* Scribners. These are good for from nine years old and upwards.

STORIES ABOUT BIBLE PEOPLE

These are very helpful because they give a background of the life and times of people in the Bible. The child's imagination is stimulated, and we try to insure against the danger of remoteness, which always threatens when we think of another civilization. The following are typical:

1. *Beggar Boy of Galilee,* JOSEPHINE S. LAU, Abingdon
    This gives vivid Palestinian background for children nine to twelve.
2. *Nathan, Boy of Capernaum,* AMY MORRIS LILLIE, Dutton
3. *Stephen,* AMY MORRIS LILLIE, Dutton
    Ten- to twelve-year-olds are much interested in these books, even when they are passing through an "indifferent" stage.

TOWARDS GREATER UNDERSTANDING

Although listed elsewhere we feel we must re-emphasize the importance of

Ways of Approach—Books

One God, FLORENCE MARY FITCH, Lothrop
   This should be read with every child as soon as he begins to show curiosity about other people's ways of worship. If he is too young for the text, we can talk to him about the pictures. It is a most remarkable book.

SOME OTHER RELIGIOUS BOOKS OF INTEREST

The Church of Our Fathers, ROLAND H. BAINTON, Scribners.
   A delightful and attractive book of Church History, illustrated with drawings from old documents. Most young people in their early teens enjoy this as a class book: unfortunately not many are sufficiently curious to want to read it alone.

The House of Prayer, FLORENCE CONVERSE. Dutton
   A clergyman once told me he had learned more about prayer from this book than from any adult one. It is old-fashioned, and best read aloud at bedtime. Timothy learns from the angel, who takes him on some wonderful expeditions. For from about eight or much older according to the thoughtfulness of the child.

St. Francis and the Animals, LEO POLITI, Scribners
   This is an example of a modern religious book for children in which first-class illustrations are used. A beautiful production.

Augustus Caesar's World, GENEVIEVE FOSTER, Scribners
   A fascinating illustrated history of the world into which Jesus was born, "a story of ideas and events from B.C. 44 to 14 A.D." The child with an enquiring mind will read it alone, others will enjoy it in class. Children tell me they like it because it tells, not only of what was happening in Palestine, but in other parts of the world.

CHAPTER ELEVEN

Disbelief

"The will-to-disbelieve is as necessary a part of our equipment as the will to believe; the two wills being indeed the same in principle but the opposite in application. The former is a weapon of defense, a protection against deceivers, never more careful than when engaged in exposing shams, fraud and cant practiced under the name of religion. The latter is a weapon of attack, the principle of all that is creative in human life. It is akin to love, the most valiant of all qualities, whether it appears in a tigress defending her cubs or in a martyr dying for mankind."

—L. P. Jacks
[*Religious Perplexities* (Doran)]

One day, just before Easter, I was conducting a junior choir practice for children from about nine to twelve years old. We had been singing some of the familiar Easter hymns and an ancient anthem called "In Joseph's Lovely Garden" which told, verse by verse, of the events of the first Easter Day. The children seemed to be very happy.

A twelve-year-old boy put up his hand, stood up, and said in an impressive voice, "My father knew a man, *and he was a minister,* and he said that women on Easter morning looked in the wrong tomb—*that's* why it was empty."

Disbelief

There was a dead silence. All the children looked enquiringly at me to see how I would answer the challenge, and I was faced with one of those occasions when you know that on your reply may hang great issues. Before me was a battery of twenty-four pairs of eyes: was this to be the moment when their owners would decide that religion is only a fairy tale after all?

With many children, the rejection of one belief is often the rejection of all belief; they know no half measures. Every parent and every teacher from time to time is faced with such crises, and on our ability to handle them lies more than we care to acknowledge. Let us consider the question in the setting where it arose. After the manner of children the boy had plunged us simply and suddenly into one of the questions about which volumes have been written and over which men have argued through the centuries. Ideally the point should have been previously met in smaller class discussions, and it might not then have been hurled at a group so varied in age and therefore in reasoning ability.

The first thing to remember is that the empty tomb part of the story is not the *important* part—the vital thing to get over in the children's own language is that the people who testified to having seen Jesus after his death had an EXPERIENCE so real and strong that the Christian Church was founded upon it. It could not have been founded upon a lie. Not everyone saw Jesus on the first Easter Day, and even those who did not recognize him at the beginning, which seems to show that it was not with ordinary human sight that they saw him, but with a keener sight that came when a certain change had taken place in them. If you look down the dim light of nearly two thousand years at the slight records in the gospels, we can see how totally unprepared these men and women were for the reappearance of Jesus. In St. Luke (24:10, 11) we read: "It was Mary Magdalene . . . and other women that were with them, which told these things unto the apostles. And their words seemed to them as idle tales, and they believed them not." In St. Mark 16, the record is twice emphasized. Mary Magdalene . . . told what she had seen to "them that had been with him, as they mourned and wept. And they, when they had heard that he was alive, and had been seen of her, believed not. After that he appeared in another form unto two of them . . . and they went and told it unto the residue: neither believed they them."

Theologians have pointed out that each of the people recorded as having had this great experience was waiting to discover, in his or her own way, the will of Jesus for their lives. Older children appreciate the specific instances of this. It was very dangerous at that particular time for Jesus' friends to keep together—it might have meant punishment for the friends of the man who had just been executed, and might put them under suspicion. Mary Magdalene was seeking Him in the garden—not His physical presence, but her mind was searching for what she could *do* for Him. And to the men on the road to Emmaus He remained a stranger *until some change took place* in them. It has been suggested that it was "when they stopped asking questions and did the Christian thing," that is, when they offered hospitality to the stranger in the breaking of bread that "their eyes were opened, and they knew him" (Luke 24:31).

To the question of the empty tomb can be applied the reasoning given a little further on in the answer to "How can we believe the gospels?"

As the boys and girls grow older they will probably meet the following arguments: The Resurrection stories were told at a time when everybody believed in miracles. Similar stories have been told about heroes in other religions. Those who argue pretend to be very scientific and regard their opponents as poor deluded beings. The danger, as we all know, is "the man who has read one book." People who argue thus have never made a deep study of comparative religions; if they had they would discover that the historians are very vague about when these miracles happened to the central figure of other religions—time is always receding when you ask for a date.

These last points are most effectively emphasized in *Asking Them Questions* [1] under the heading, "Can You Prove that the Story of the Resurrection Is True?" "We can date, as a scientific fact," says Rev. George F. MacLeod, who happens to answer that question, "when His Church was growing by leaps and bounds—inspired in its splendid faith solely by a conviction of the Resurrection. And the time that elapsed between His death and the coming of His Church is so short that it precludes absolutely the possibility that the vitality of the Church in the first century was based on a 'hoax legend.' "

The above-mentioned book is of great value to teachers and parents. The editor tells in the preface how one night after the usual service in the Chapel of the St. Giles' Cathedral Club in Edinburgh, Scotland, he asked each boy to write any question about the Christian faith that perplexed him. He says every question in the book was asked by an actual boy, not over eighteen, and a member of their club and Scout troop. He says:

"The questions came to me as a revelation of just what the boys are thinking. 'Fancy asking questions like that,'

[1] Ed. by Ronald Selby Wright, pp. 131, p. V, Oxford University Press.

I said . . . 'so he does think about other things besides football and swimming.' A telegraph messenger asked, 'What was Christ's position to God if he prayed to God?' an apprentice plumber about the 'Second Coming'; a butcher's messenger boy about the Trinity; a young gardener about the Soul; one schoolboy about the Vision of God . . . and so on. More than half the questions were about subjects like Heaven and Hell, evil, sin, and suffering (involving the extent of the power of God), and the relation of Jesus Christ to God.

"I saw at once the mistake we in our Clubs . . . often make, of presenting to our boys a vague and sentimental watered-down religion, as if the Christian religion were *merely* 'living a decent life, keeping fit, helping others, and all that sort of thing.' "

The book is made up of answers to the boys' questions written by eminent religious authorities. Examples of these are:

How can God be everywhere at the same time?
If God made everything, who made evil?
What is meant by the Kingdom of God?
Why does God permit such happenings as earthquakes?
Why should I love God?
Can you prove that Jesus lived: historically?
What evidence has the church for calling Christ God?
Why call Him more than a fine man?
Does God really take any notice of our prayers?
What is the soul?
Is there a Hell?
What is sin?
Where is Heaven?

Readers may be interested in the type of question asked, a few months before this chapter was written, by twelve-year-old boys in a church school in this country. I asked the successful teacher of these lively boys—a man who has the gift of meeting them on their own ground in their own language —to give me a few typical questions he had been asked during the past year, and his method of answering them. The following is what I received:

PREVENTIVE MEDICINE

Disease: We can't believe the Bible because some things in it obviously aren't true. The story of the creation in Genesis we know isn't so. We should look for our information to men of science, like Darwin, for instance, who taught us that men are descended from monkeys.

Treatment: Darwin's *Origin of Species* brought into class with side comment that Scopes was convicted for teaching evolution in Tennessee (with as much detail as the boys wanted) but here we're not afraid of the truth—we seek it. For the truth, let's look at what Darwin did say. Boys who supposedly quoted from Darwin were challenged to find the statement concerning descent from monkeys and of course could not. Pointed out that, throughout the book, Darwin refers frequently and respectfully to "the Creator." What Darwin really did was not to challenge the idea that God created the world, but to attempt to explain how He did it and, to some extent, how long it may have taken to do it. Darwin necessarily did this by putting down what he knew and then trying to explain what he was sure of by ideas which he thought fit the facts—ideas as to how different animals developed and changed as different features enabled certain ones to grow strong and survive. We will have no trouble with Genesis if we realize that the man who wrote Genesis, how long before Christ we don't know, was trying to do somewhat the same thing—to tell the story of the creation as best he could in the light of what he knew. He didn't know a lot of things we do, but if we are fair to him, we can see that he did a pretty good job without too much to go on. And if we just substitute "period" for the word "day," which was a different word in Greek or Hebrew anyway, there is little to trouble us. Even the detail that man is made of "dust" is true, for he is indeed made of dirt—i.e. different kinds of matter—and lots of water! But there is more to him than that—which is the fascinating mystery of life and his soul and where man is going anyhow—and that's where God comes in. No other idea makes any sense in the light of the things we know to be so, for all this development must have some reason and something it is trying to do—some place it is trying to go.

Related squawk: How can we believe the gospels? We know they were not written during the life of Christ, and they differ. Are any of them reliable, and if so, which one?

Discussion: As a preliminary, examine sources of information we readily accept now: books, magazines, newspapers—all written by people some of whom describe things they have seen themselves, but many of whom discuss matters far beyond their personal experience, yet rely on the word of others for facts. We are by no means as critical of gossip, of supposedly true news of the day or of many historical events which we believe occurred as our sceptics would have us be of the Bible. Obviously Jesus was not followed about by a stenographer—nobody was then. But what He did and said made a deep impression on those who saw and heard Him, and when it was realized how important these matters were and that He would not soon reappear in person, they were written down with great care, just as we write, say, a history of World War I, by combining what we do remember with what others can tell us and what they noted down. As to why we have four gospels, teacher put on an act supposedly from the "March of Time," consisting of the biography of Ernie Blabbermouth, who threw his food out of his high-chair at three, made gliders and spitballs in Sunday school because he knew more than teacher, loafed, behatted and smoked at his job because he knew more than the boss, but finally had to confess to his golden-haired granddaughter that he never got anywhere—although, of course, he knew more than anyone else. Boys were then asked to write down what they had seen and heard, answers (by permission) read aloud. Pointed out that there was no question that what they had written about happened, and each boy's account was substantially correct, but all were different.

Cliché: Christianity, when you get right down to it, is just like a lot of other Oriental religions—it grew out of them, resembles them, and is nothing but a modern rationalization of primitive stuff (children won't put it that way, but in general this is what they mean—they've heard it). There is really little difference in the teachings of Jesus, who just put the old Jewish beliefs into new words—or indeed between teachings of Jesus and Confucius, who didn't pretend to be a deity at all.

Approach: After some study of various teachings in the Bible, it is fun to bring in Confucius without saying who it is, and to read, and ask the children to guess who said, things like this: "The Master said . . . not to do unto others what we would not they should do unto us"—"Exalt the straight, put aside the crooked; the crooked will grow straight."—"Who cannot rule himself, how should he rule others?" The more we study the minds of the great, the more frequently we find how many ideas they had in common. It does not matter too much whether Jesus knew what Confucius said or not—perhaps he knew a little, for we probably underestimate his unspecified education. But Jesus was no parrot. He put the Golden Rule in a positive form.

Children and Religion

When asked what the fundamental law was, he did not quote the Ten Commandments, full of "Thou shalt not." He said we should love God and our neighbor—again an accurate summary of the Jewish teaching, but newly combined, newly phrased, into a positive, hopeful fundamental that might be a key to the most simple or the most complicated life—easy to understand, hard to do. Jesus encouraged every possible revolt against the forms of the old practices, got into trouble for challenging them, kept insisting that the old sacrifices, the old set ways, were not enough. He alone beckons the world to a new life, a new way, confidence in the individual, love for enemy as well as friend, forgiveness and kindness and understanding, and an immortality of the spirit. He was such an innovator that we have yet to demonstrate that we can follow His leadership.

Canard: Jesus' teachings may have sounded all right sometime but they don't make sense in our modern world. They were too idealistic to apply to a man who has to make a living in the world as he finds it.

Attack: This is a tough one—it sneaks up on all of us. However, we should remember that Jesus' teachings were utterly revolutionary in His own time. Nevertheless, they offer a possible solution to human problems of all time— which is why they survive. Probably none of us can be sure just how "impractical" He wanted everybody to be. It is not fair, intellectually or to Jesus, to lift what He said from its context and say of a phrase: this was His teaching. He told the rich to give away what they had and follow Him, the laggard not to bury his dead, and so on. But the Bible tells us man must live by the sweat of his brow, and there is no praise for a loafer. Jesus points out that no father, asked for bread, will give a stone, and the parable of the wise and foolish virgins certainly encourages some preparedness for practical problems. But Jesus certainly kept hammering at the idea that a man preoccupied by what he considered the material necessities of this life was headed for trouble. Illustration used to persuade the young: Pictures of the Collyer brothers, in *Life,* who hoarded all kinds of junk for fear they'd starve or have things stolen. Result: no friends, no fun, apprehension with every meal, one died and the police discovered that the other brother had been killed by a trap he had set to catch prowlers.

A very clear example of religious perplexity came to my notice recently, a nine-year-old child whose doctor-mother is very anxious that she shall have a "scientific" attitude toward everything. From time to time she spends the weekend with her grandfather who reads to her from an excellent book of Bible stories, among which are some stories of the Creation. Various factors may have contributed to the dispirited condition in which she arrived on one of these weekend visits, but I think there had been an especially earnest and recent campaign conducted by her mother, for quite early in the day she announced that the stories she'd heard on previous visits "weren't true." Later her grandfather was showing her some postcards, one of which was a picture of people in Australia eating their Christmas dinner as a picnic outside in the blazing sun. The little girl looked up politely and then said, "But of course it isn't true. Christmas couldn't come in the summer."

How can we help the child who is beginning to think there is *nothing* we can believe in? In this particular case, when the Creation stories were read, they should have been emphasized as those handed down for a great many years, perhaps told round the camp fires, great poems trying to express how the world was made. Actually as the years go on, they do tie in more closely with the discoveries of science, but mystery remains. With this in mind she would not have had such a strong conflict with her grandfather's ideas. She should also have been told that some of the stories had an historic basis.

Too often this conflict occurs in the same way between the teaching or casual comments received at home, and that of the Sunday school. The prevention of this is one of the primary reasons for undertaking to establish co-operation between the two, which cannot be too strongly emphasized. It is not exaggeration to say that a few words from a parent— so often to a child an infallible authority—are enough to alter the whole trend of the young religious life; for children have not formed the habit of evaluating opinions. There is plenty to offer in teaching religion that we need not quarrel about; so much of the Bible, for example, the historicity of which is no longer doubted by reliable scholars. If the parents have delved into some of the books on the Bible suggested in Chapter Ten, and better still, if their inquisitive minds have led them into deeper investigation in theological libraries, they will not make the glib statement we hear on every side, "Every liberal-minded person knows the Bible is made up of myths."

It would seem best, in the case of the disillusioned child, to lead towards those simple realities of which we can be *certain*. The following verse, although not great poetry, the child can grasp:

> O God, whose laws will never change,
> We thank you for these things we know;
> That after rain the sun will shine,
> That after darkness light appears,
> That winter always brings the spring,
> That after sleep we wake again,
> That life goes on, and love remains,
> And life and love can never die.

Then the child should be guided to bind together other abiding things we can tell him of—for example, by studying the life and character of Jesus we become aware of the *certainty* of His love for mankind, and of his continuing Presence.

There was another child whose parents had a vital religious life and an insight into the function of Christianity in the world today. These qualities had helped them to found a healthy religious life in their child. At Sunday dinner there would be some religious discussion, and the conversation would be apt to take a critical turn which, although usually harmless in front of an older child or between adults, is confusing to the very young. The talk would proceed on these lines:

> Father: It was a good sermon this morning.
> Mother: I felt it wandered unnecessarily. If the minister had stuck to the three points he was making on the types of intercession, it would have been much more impressive.
> Father: Maybe. He certainly quoted too much.
> Mother: I know: there were about five places where he could have stopped. Each would have been perfect, and he'd have left the thing clear in our minds.
> Father: Well, you can't expect perfection. He gives us a pretty good nugget to take away every week.
> Mother: That anthem by Schubert today was fine, but I thought it was just a shade flat in the second half when the sopranos took over. . . .

The adolescent having reached the stage when he loves nothing better than to analyze everything himself, might even have been helped by such a conversation. His estimation of parental intelligence might even go up a little; they are not so blind after all, but that they can see room for improvement although they do respect the Church and continue to give of themselves to work and worship in it. There must be a great deal to religion, whatever the others at school say about it. But your little child is baffled—the more so if he is of the sensitive kind: all he gets out of the dialogue is the erroneous impression that Mummy and Daddy don't like what goes on in church. Then there must be something wrong with church and church school.

In the case cited here, the child began to lose interest in attending the church school, and then finally begged not to go. The parents upon investigation found that excellent and interesting teaching was being offered, but they had failed to keep in touch with the planned courses. On several occasions when they asked the child casually "what he had done to-day," their raised eyebrows and comment, "How strange! Why do they do *that* in your class?" together with the kind of mealtime conversation indicated, had gradually built up in the child's mind the idea that church and all its works were pretty queer and not really approved of by his trusted parents. Fortunately the root of the matter was found because the parents cared and had no idea what they were doing. Interest was slowly rebuilt. The mother came to one or two classes to prove her loyalty, and informed herself on what was happening. Criticism above the child's head was left for the occasions when he was not there. This, of course, does not mean that you give the impression that the world is a garden of perfection, and if Johnny Jones hits your child on the head, and your child smudges Johnny's drawing, it is of no use glossing over the episode. Such things he meets in his own world, but we need not add to his problems by arguing the minister's histrionic ability.

Disbelief

Another common question to be faced by us all, and through which come graver doubts in the young child, is *"Is there really a Santa Claus?"*

It is startling when talking to older people to discover how many have had the seeds of disillusionment sown in the Santa Claus myth. As we saw in the earlier chapters, the little child lives half in and half out of fairyland, and there is but a thin veil between fact and fancy. I do not think it is fair for grown-ups to teach Santa Claus as an historic fact, because, irreverent as it may sound, they do put him on a par with Jesus, and the fantastic truth is that in the child's mind the two often stand and fall together. Not many parents nowadays derive satisfaction from teaching their children that babies are brought by storks, or try to preserve that state of "innocence" as long as possible; but they do continue to wink at each other and describe how Santa Claus comes down the chimney, and to tell Santa Claus stories with the same tone of conviction that they use when speaking of the Nativity. This is done to such an extent that children will tell their teachers very frequently that "Christmas is Santa Claus' birthday." No doubt many outgrow the secular ideas of Christmas, but many do not. There is little wisdom in adding to the many perplexities they will inevitably meet: the fantasy cannot last for long in this rationalistic age, and those who wish to keep up the idea of Santa Claus as a living person will have to pile one lie on top of another. Very early the child will announce that the chimney is too small for a man, and enquire how Santa Claus manages to visit every child in the world in one evening, and so on.

Because Christmas is one of the high points of the year, we naturally want it to be happy for the entire family, and half the reason for wanting to establish Santa Claus as a fact is that the grown-ups want their share of the fun! We can have it. When the child is very young we can all "play Santa Claus" together, then as soon as he is old enough for a good "once upon a time" story, (not too soon) we should read up on Saint Nicholas himself—again the public library will yield assistance. Tell the story of Saint Nicholas, and show how it grew up in our own country. Most of us know that the popular saint was a very rich man (some say a bishop) who wanted to help all his friends by giving them bags of money when they were in need, but because he hated thanks, always tried to give his presents secretly. When a friend of his was in great want, he threw a purse of gold down the chimney of the needy family, say the legends—in this case to provide a dowry for the beautiful daughter. These legends grew up all over Europe. The good man was canonized, so they probably weren't legends after all—and he was given his special day— December 6th. Different countries have different versions of his benevolent deeds, and many countries—especially the Dutch—took him to their hearts: their "Sinter Claus" became our "Santa Claus" when the Netherlanders settled in this country. And we in turn made our versions of what he looked like and what he did, and how he traveled. You will not give all of this to the small child, of course; the main thing is to keep Santa Claus as we know him today a "pretend" person belonging to the play world, and Jesus a real person belonging to all the world forever. They will be inevitably close when the child is very young, but help him not to keep them on the same plane as he grows. And when we get our book of legends and tell about St. Nicholas, we should also try to have our children know of the Christmas customs of other countries, and to sing carols from other lands. Some families even try to combine a few European customs with our own, beginning many days before Christmas, but this idea is not acceptable to many.

So I believe we should all *play* at being Santa Claus, and the reality will remain in doing kind things for other people —a celebration of kindness, in fact. Parents join in the play and have their special ritual of stocking-filling and other delights. If we are realistic we must face the fact that Billy next door may have parents who are trying to present Santa Claus as a living person, and rack our brains for the best way to meet this exigency.

A question closely related to this, and which almost always arises in the child's mind, is *"Did Jesus really work miracles?"*

The danger of telling miracles to little children lies in their acceptance of them as a kind of magic. It is not at all uncommon to have primary children proffer accounts of how they saw a magician at a show doing this or that, just after a miracle story has been told.

It is easier to *reason* about miracles with older classes than with primary children. Some believe that the telling of miracle stories should be strictly limited with these little ones, and those that are told should be the ones revealing the *character* of Jesus, His service of others and what some may call His "secret power" (which came from God) of helping the sick and the unhappy. This idea works out very well if we are the only people choosing what the child will hear, but we cannot guard our children constantly, hanging labels round their necks. "Please do not tell Bible stories to this child without consulting me." We saw that in the account previously given of the boy hearing about the Crucifixion (Chap. 3). Moreover they will almost certainly meet those casually chosen books of Bible stories, receive them as gifts, and find them in houses where they stay. They will hear about the stilling of the storm, and the walking on the water, and they may also hear the older boy who says, "I don't believe a word of it."

In combatting the idea of magic, or conjuring tricks, point out the times when Jesus refused to perform miracles at all. *When they were performed, it was to teach men more about God.* The stories of the Temptation show very clearly that He would not perform miracles just to "show off." Jesus wanted to show our unbelieving world how God can break into our lives with His power, if we make way for Him. Again, children, when studying the events of the Crucifixion often ask, "Why didn't Jesus save Himself? He could have." It is almost as if they are a little disappointed, because their movie heroes and the strong man of the funny papers always escape at the last minute. Children can be led to see that the giving of Himself was the most shining of all miracles. He would not use His power to prevent this self-giving to all men, and His coming back to prove victory over death itself. Dr. Fosdick in his book, *On Being Fit to Live With,* tells how a fourteen-year-old boy in a church school volunteered the answer to "Why did Jesus have to die?" The boy said, "Jesus saw a lot of good in this world, and He didn't like the way it was being pushed around, somebody had to take the rap, and He took it."

The experience of those trying to answer religious questions in different times and in different countries has emphasized the similarity in the perplexities of all sorts and conditions of men. The tragedy lies in the fact that these questions so often lie *unanswered* in people's minds to the extent of stunting and sometimes extinguishing their religious life. They escape to unworthy resources, forgetting the day when burning curiosity might have led them somewhere. If they would turn to other sources, it might be possible to grow instead of remaining in a spiritual childhood. Chaplains in the armed forces have testified to this over and over again. Ministers support their conclusions. Nearly every minister can give a list of questions he is asked continually, and excuses he is constantly offered, such as, "I keep away from religion and I find my life is as good as those who don't," "How can there be a God when He lets all these horrors happen?" and "I was sent to church too much as a child, so I don't go now."

Much confusion comes through the religious idiom. An elderly lady came up to the speaker after a religious talk and confided, "Do you know, when I was a child, I always thought God was very fat."

"Really," said the speaker, "why was that?"

"Because I heard Him described as 'Three Persons in One God.'" I happen to know that that lady has outgrown her infantile conceptions of the deity, but many are still floundering at the point.

Not long after I was present at the above incident, a very fine man said to me, "You know, I don't go to church very often because I simply can't swallow the idea of cutting God into three pieces."

Ministers are trained to help such people as these. Their studies have led them to face these problems. Although men and women never solve them completely on this planet, if we do in fact wish to be honest and are not using shallow remarks as an escape or an excuse for not changing our way of life or shouldering inevitable responsibilities, we must come out into the open and expose ourselves to straightforward argument as a scientist would do, taking care not to seek out only those who will be likely to agree with us.

The religious curiosity of many people stops at High School

level or earlier, and they do not exert themselves to satisfy what is there. The condemnations and destructive criticisms used at "bull sessions" in the late teens and early twenties remain the stock-in-trade to the end of our lives if we stop growing. Perhaps the best people to talk to, besides those whose minds are trained along the lines we are exploring, are the ones who have made their faith *work,* and who by the dynamic quality of their lives show that they derive strength and inspiration from a dynamic faith.

I think there is much help to be had in a little book by L. P. Jacks called *Religious Perplexities,* in which are three profound lectures: "The Source of Perplexity," "Religious Perplexity in General," and "Perplexity in the Christian Religion." Professor Jacks warns that religion, like loyalty, or grief, or the love of man and woman, is cheapened by over-defense and when cheapened it can become incredible. He feels that religion has suffered as much from its would-be friends as its would-be enemies.

"Christianity," he says, "in the official, or authorized presentation of it, is a *smothered* religion: smothered almost to the point of total asphyxiation and collapse, but not quite; smothered by the vested interests of great institutions, and by the ambitions, fears, and self-seekings that such interests breed; smothered by the elaborate theological defenses that Christians have built, not against Antichrist, but against each other; smothered in these anxieties, not unnatural in these embroilments, for its own future. If you take Christianity along with its entanglements, encumbrances and unnatural alliances; if you present it with all the secular baggage which the ages have fastened upon it, you will then find it a hopelessly perplexing thing, a thing which neither Reason nor Faith, whether acting singly or in combination, can accept.

"But alongside the authorized version, and sometimes hidden within it as an inextinguishable spark of life, Christianity has an unauthorized version, which the former has often repressed, persecuted and condemned to the hangman or to the eternal flames. Of this unauthorized version a fair copy exists in the hearts of men, a fairer copy in the hearts of women, and the fairest of all in the hearts of children—for Christianity is pre-eminently a religion of the young. It is the unauthorized version which has kept Christianity alive through the ages and defied the smotherers even to this day. . . .

"Something to talk about, something worth talking about, was furnished before the talking began. . . . There we touch the dynamic principle of Christianity, cut free from its entanglements with a mass of things that do not belong to it; the power which still keeps it alive under a mountain of verbal accretions that would smother anything less divine. In the beginning was the deed; go thou and do likewise. So presented, Christianity is not perplexing; but quite the most convincing religion ever offered either to the intellect or the heart. The perplexities have arisen from the reversal of the true order; from the attempt to subordinate the things done to the things said; to lay the foundations in argument and propaganda which can only be laid in actual performance; . . . when theology gets the upper hand of religion. The deeds that I do, these bear witness of me. What other conceivable witness could there be?"

If we can lead our children to see that Jesus was not always preaching, that he was *living* His teaching, and if we try to direct their hearts and minds to the central realities, there will be more chance of our keeping alive in them a lasting faith in God.

BOOKS ON CHRISTIAN BELIEF

FOR TEENAGERS (ANSWERS TO QUESTIONS)

KNIGHT and HAWKES, *There's an Answer Somewhere*, Longmans
JONES, G. CURTIS, *Youth Deserves to Know*, Macmillan
CHAPLIN, DORA P., *We Want to Know*, Morehouse
WRIGHT, RONALD S., *Asking Them Questions*, Third Series, Oxford
FINEGAN, J., *Youth Asks About Religion*, Assoc. Press
By Prominent   *Moral Problems*
Anglican Churchmen.   *Difficulties.* Both paperbacks, published by
                      Mowbray (Obtainable through
                      Morehouse)

MORE GENERAL BOOKS ON BELIEF

FOR TEACHERS, PARENTS, AND OLDER TEENAGERS

READ, DAVID H. C., *The Christian Faith*, Scribners
WHALE, J. S., *Christian Doctrine*, Cambridge University Press
PHILLIPS, J. B., *Your God is Too Small*, Macmillan
CASSERLEY, J. V. L., *No Faith of My Own*, Longmans
PIKE, JAMES A., *Beyond Anxiety*, Scribners

CHAPTER TWELVE

Experience of God

"It has taken all the philosophical and spiritual travail of the centuries to think through the idea of a concrete Infinite, interrelated with us and with the world, and to discover that the way to share in His immanent and comprehending Life is as much a way of affirmation as of negation. Mysticism will not be revived and become a powerful present-day force until it is liberated from dependence on outworn and inadequate forms, and until it conquers for itself more congenial thought—terms through which in a vital way it can translate its human experience and its vision of God."

—RUFUS JONES
[In "Prayer and the Mystic Vision,"
From *Concerning Prayer*, Macmillan. By permission]

"Lord, make us apt to teach, but more apt to learn, that we may desire not only to reveal to others what Thou hast revealed to us, but with open and hospitable minds to learn of them what they have learned of their world and of Thee. Amen."

"Daily Prayer" from
[*Prayers for Private Devotions in Wartime*.
Oxford University Press]

We have tried to see our position, as parents and teachers, in a civilization that has science and politics without

vision. We believe that peace is possible only by the understanding of spiritual power, and that education today, lacking in Christian attitudes, gives our children no sustaining
strength for their life in a tragic world. In this little book
we have tried for a brief time to discover what conditions
are likely to be best for the education of the spirit, in the
search for a spiritual reality that will, through integrated
lives, help to build an integrated world.

We touched very lightly on the trends of psychology and
its relation to the religious life of the child, realizing the
scope and depth of the subject which has been rightly called
"human wisdom's youngest child," and we have at different
stages considered books likely to be helpful to parents and
teachers, who realize that the laws at work in the growth
of human personality are the laws of God. Our teaching must
be in line with the natural growth of the child's mind, otherwise no amount of "piety" will make our attempts creative.

We looked rather more closely into the needs of different
ages, and considered the relation of the home to the growth
of the child. Opportunities for religious teaching during the
Christian festivals of Easter and Christmas seemed especially
important, and other major events of the Christian year, which
should also be remembered in the home. See Anne Proctor,
The Christian Household (Longmans). Then, thinking of
prayer as life in God, we tried to understand how to teach
the child to pray, thinking of prayer at home, in company
with others, and silent prayer. Because the problem of the
child's attitude toward death so frequently confronts us, we
gave time to finding how we could help the bereaved child,
or the child who meets death in any form.

In Chapter Seven we wondered if church schools should
exist at all, what they could be, and what they offer. The

three following chapters were devoted to ways of approaching religion through Bible study, and the relation of art and literature to religion, giving practical list of books and other material. We faced some of the common perplexities met by most children and some adults.

Finally, we can look at some central facts and our ability to meet them. One good way to begin to understand the children we teach is to look backward and examine the religion of our own childhood, trying to remember how we felt at a certain age, and giving some thought to the methods—chance methods or formal ones—by which we acquired what religious ideas we possess. Our duty lies in helping children to retain and develop their natural powers of religious perception. We dare not leave this important side of human life to chance, while we expend endless time, money and effort on everything else. Our work with children will not be fruitful unless we enrich and deepen our own vision of God, resisting the temptation to use "outworn and inadequate forms and expressions," hackneyed religious phrases which we expect the child to understand.

We have, moreover, to help the children to find God in *ordinary* life. Very few of us are called to exciting worldly adventures. The majority of the children we teach will be homemakers and bread winners, they will lead busy, often driven lives, feeling the impact of whatever shakes the world in the birth of a new civilization. Now, more than ever, do we need to build on rock. "They are not," says Evelyn Underhill in her paper, "The Teacher's Vocation," "going to be people with special powers of spiritual devotion, able to use long periods of prayer, even if they had time for them. Hence it is very important to make them realize now that Christian communion with God takes many outward forms; that there is no outward act, no kind of work, no drudgery, joy, suffering, which cannot be turned into a means of intercourse, a virtual prayer, provided it is accepted from the hand of God in a spirit of love; that He will come to them incessantly in the train and the office, the shop, the factory, the home; perpetually offering something which, faithfully accepted, will become real food for their souls. It is your greatest privilege to teach your children to recognize this. Teach them the sense of God's nearness, and of His constant sheltering, moulding, strengthening, feeding Presence with each separate life."

The traditional way to educate a child in religion was the transmissive way: this method was used far back in the centuries, probably as soon as any attempt at formal religious education was begun; it was certainly used long before the birth of Christ, and has been carried on through the life of the Christian church. In many places this approach is still popular. The child learns by rote hymns, prayers, and passages from the Bible, he repeats creeds, and in some cases has to learn by heart the answers to a set of religious questions. It has taken us a long time to learn that religious instruction and religious education are not the same thing. There are many arguments for and against this way of teaching. We need adults—both teachers and parents, who have themselves learned to apply dogma to life, and are able to guide the children. It has been followed by a number of other theories, ranging from a purely subjective approach, found in many Protestant churches, and often ending in a luke-warm, conventional goodness as a goal, to the purely objective one, stressing worship as its main theme, and the continued praise of God.

In 1939 Archbishop Temple is said to have remarked, "The world is in its present chaotic state, not because a great many people are very wicked, but because they are just like us."

Experience of God

We want our children to outgrow us spiritually. Unfortunately many adults have never outgrown their childish ideas of God. In dealing with numbers of children, one becomes aware that it is usually possible to discover the parents' ideas of God from those the child possesses. Some of the extraordinary ideas of God some children have could never exist if their family had grown up in religion.

There is a poem about a little boy:

> Who paced and dug his garden plot
> And prayed unto his little God—
> And when the universe grew great
> He dreamed for it a greater God . . .

It is our task to help him to discover that greater God, but we need not "dream Him," for He is.

As we move about the world we hear of a variety of religious experiences which have befallen our fellow men and women in their childhood. Some people were so frightened or bored by these incidents, or they were of such a nature that as their intellects grew they had to reject them altogether. Or some belonged to the "advanced" type of parents who said rather proudly, "We're not going to send Johnny to any church. When he is old enough he can decide for himself." (How? Would you ask his opinion on the Differential Calculus before he could do simple addition?)

We meet others who tell us that in spite of mistakes and boredom, they had a feeling that God was *important* to their parents, that religion was real to them, that it influenced their lives and characters in a way that demanded respect, so that in later years they found themselves looking for such an influence themselves; they were hungry for ideas in a world concerning itself chiefly with things.

We must remember that the child growing up in the world

of today often differs from the young people of even a decade ago—some of the hurry and uncertainty of our time seems to have got into his system. Ask any teacher who has taught for twenty years, even in a district where there is no financial stress, and he will probably tell you that our children are more nervous and more self-opinionated than their predecessors, that they are unstable, have a poor sense of values, and above all that most of them actively resist work which demands from them even a little concentration and mental discipline. A teacher in a famous Sunday school told me recently that their staff was beginning to suspect that the pupils came there to be entertained.

Whether we consider the child of yesterday or today, we find three potent factors at work, whether we are aware of it or not: The attitudes, behavior, and even the casual conversations of adults; formal teaching on religion; and, most important of all, the natural desire of the child to reach out to God.

All these factors belong to the home as well as to the church school and day school. Religious education given in the Sunday school is only a supplement to, not a substitute for, the home influence, neither is it a new thing, it is going on every minute of the child's waking life: the Eastern poet calls religion "all deeds and all reflection," so how can we confine it to Sunday alone?

As we go more deeply into the study of the Christian education of our children, we see that contrary to the opinion held by most psychologists in our own childhood, many modern psychologists of standing give us their support in our quest for the spiritual life; in this we owe a great debt to psychology, which in many quarters now contends that only experience of God as revealed in Jesus Christ can meet the needs of healthy growing minds. A tremendous responsibility is thus placed upon us. Whether we like it or not, and whether we are aware of it or not, the little child gets his first ideas of God through his parents. We hope he will go further than we have gone; meanwhile he must witness the love of God through ourselves; those ideas of parental personality are sinking deep into the recesses of the spirit. The atmosphere of the home is said to depend on three things—the attitude of the parents towards each other, towards the child, and towards God. In other words, the child will unconsciously see the depth and reality of our own religious lives.

Now the exciting thing about all this is the way it opens new doors for the parents themselves. In retracing our steps to go along with a child (only do not be surprised if you find the child leading you) it so often happens that we ourselves find a new experience of God—it is one of the most thrilling experiences that can happen to any human being. Our refusal to change our own way of life, or perhaps our own uncertainty, is sometimes a reason for not starting out on the journey. The fact remains that many wise people go so far as to say that up to the age of about three years in the child's life, the parents fill the place of God!

Of later childhood Basil A. Yeaxlee [1] says: "The truth about God may be obscured or distorted in the experience of a child if his parents are in their relationship with him weak, unwise, inconsistent, sentimentally indulgent, hard, overbearing, careless or indifferent, *whatever beliefs about God they may profess or try to teach the child.* On the other hand, if they are in any sense parents they will inevitably mediate to him (and not simply illustrate) the fact that God is, and the meaning and the power of God the Father everlasting."

The young child has potential evil within him, and infinite

[1] *Religion and the Growing Mind,* p. 80, Seabury Press.

possibilities of good; or as one mother of four lively little boys proclaimed, the normal child is a combination of devil and angel, the devil frequently appearing uppermost, but it is the job of parents to see that the angel wins in the end.

Most children respond satisfactorily to our effort to let the angel win the game, so we start off with the good word on our side, or, if we want more scholarly language, Professor Pratt tells us that "a truly religious attitude is natural to him [the child] because he possesses those instincts which in their combination made the adult man religious." But we want to clear our minds, and in the hurry-scurry of our lives, have fixed stars to steer by.

"What books shall I get for my little boy? You know, I'm so helpless about knowing what to tell him about God, and he asks so many questions. I'm not sure about these things myself—it is just the blind leading the blind." People who talk that way are half-way there already. You know, Pascal said there are only two kinds of people one calls reasonable —"either those who serve God with all their hearts because they know Him, or those who search after Him with all their heart because they do not know Him." The self-satisfied ones are the only ones it seems impossible to help, but even they are often rescued by their children.

Parents and teachers, who in all sincerity want to include the search for true religion in their plans to help the intelligent growth of those in their care fall into two groups, not unlike those defined by Pascal, those who, having a very real religious life of their own want to pass it on, and those who, having become parents, or having seen the urgent necessity for helping their pupils to a wider life, suddenly realize that they need to find a faith to share with their children.

The first group will have discovered that they have explored higher levels of life than those on which men generally live, but they will be looking for new ways of interpretation; the second group are on a voyage of discovery, and we can all travel along together. At first we are largely concerned with the comments of the beginners: all the mistakes and missing links in our education they bring back to us— almost always there have been unhappy religious experiences which have stunted their growing up in religious ideas; or they hated Sunday school and despised their teachers; those who taught them didn't practice what they preached; or they were forced to go to church so often that when they were allowed to manage their own lives they never went again. All these are very common statements, we have them all by heart. Just a few of our fellow-travelers tell us that they belong to the Lost Generation, their parents belonged to the *laissez-faire* set, and as their eyes become opened by the higher criticism of the Bible, their cry of "freedom for religion" became, without their realizing it, "freedom from religion."

Although we may be teaching pious or so-called religious subjects, we are not necessarily helping the child to grow nearer to his God. Religion cannot be communicated through the printed page. Many people receive careful training before attempting to teach other subjects. In most states a hairdresser must have a certificate to show his skill before practicing his complicated "art"; but anyone can "teach Sunday school," as we blithely say, and alas they do.

"To educate a child in religion," says an old book, "requires quietude of mind." "Thou hast need," says the poet, "to busy thine heart with quietude." In our day we are almost afraid of silence, and when the noise around us ceases we are disquieted. God is waiting for us, but we do not stop to listen. William Hocking says, "A man's ultimate relations are solely to God, and perhaps the deepest thing in Christianity is the adequacy with which it presents the ultimate solitude of the soul, not alone in birth, or in death, but in the history of its own ethical problem, which no man can meet for it."

It would seem that the essential thing is that either religion should be an integral part of the family life; or the *search* for it should be normal, and above all real and important. If we examine our ways and words very carefully, we may be shocked at where we place our emphasis. Does the child unconsciously feel that the parents think knowing the right people, being on the baseball team at school, or winning many badges at Scouts more important than God? And when we use His Name, do we sound a little self-conscious and use a rather pious tone of voice? Is religion crowded out of life by the other more "important" things? If so, it is of no use our paying lip service to it—the children will know.

It seems evident that the attainment of maturity is what we want for our children, and in looking toward it we see them wrestling with the normal pattern of human development: first, the little child, eagerly accepting everything; then, as he grows, he stands back and looks at himself with growing self-consciousness. He looks at himself in relation to his environment, and he becomes critical. This has been likened to the posting of a censor at the gateway of his five senses which have hitherto given him only a happy receptivity, and we call this egocentric period adolescence. Then should come maturity, the time when unselfconsciousness returns, because the individual has forgotten himself—he trusts again because he is sure, not of himself, but of God. This is the "rebirth" taught by Christianity. Too many in this present civilization remained obsessed with self, and never reach the last stage. Only those who have achieved it are qualified to teach children, for otherwise, how can they go all the way with them?

At a meeting of parents a headmaster recently pointed out that our schools, and he feared many of our homes, are filled with people who have not grown up. "They are still," he said, "in the adolescent stage of self-centeredness, criticism and prejudice. They have, too, the adolescent's itch to throw their weight about and dominate, and that is their method of dealing with their young charges. They often," he went on, "announce that they are 'good with children,' and I learned long ago to be shy of individuals who made that claim for themselves. They are, it may be added, often possessed of great intellectual gifts, but their effect upon children is always ultimately disastrous, for the gulf between the adolescent and childhood is wide and deep. These folk, however devoted they may be to their work, direct their children from the other side of an impassable rift, and children cannot be directed—they can only be led. To lead them we must have hold of their hands, and if we are to do that there must be no gulf between us." [2] We can take our warning from such a statement and look to our own equipment for the task before us. Have we patience enough, when we know we may never see the results of our long labors?

We want to make all education part of Christian education, for so it is, in so far as it widens the child's horizon and enriches his universe. We must never cease to remind ourselves that imparting pieces of information is only a part of our task. Every teacher has been called an artist in human life, and, if we are to live up to this ideal, we must give significance to all other knowledge by allying it to the creative

[2] Geoffrey Hoyland, "The Re-birth of the Adult." *Parent's Review,* Jan. 1947.

will of God. It is my belief that a little child has a simple capacity for drawing close to God, for perceiving spiritual reality; and in our adult clumsiness we dwarf his growing spiritual life. We have referred repeatedly to the acute perception shown by children, and how they manage in a few words to show knowledge of some great truth.

"Thank you for the friends we make," said a five-year-old girl saying part of "A Child's Grace." Then she stopped suddenly and said to me, "We don't make our friends, do we? But we do make our love for them." We offer them their little rhymes, not knowing how the enquiring intelligence is brooding over the words.

I believe that however much religious teaching a child receives, unless he can be prepared for a real religious experience, his life is just as empty as before. Every individual must find his own road to God. Aristotle's words on education might be applied especially to religious education, "About the means there is no agreement; for different persons, starting with different ideas about the nature of virtue, naturally disagree about the practice of it." We have referred in Chapter Four to the effect in adolescence of experiences of high objective delight. In this country, one of the places we must not fail is in giving our children, in camps and by other means, opportunity to delight in the natural beauty of the outdoor world.

But young people seem to need the smaller, quieter gatherings, as well as the noisy hilarity of bigger assemblies, and they need solitude. Pity those who only rush about in cars, their eyes glued to the map, or looking ahead to the next movie theater or eating place, and who at the end can boast of little more than the mileage covered. In the appreciation of nature we are tied in some measure to our inner life, for

Experience of God

the calm and clarity of thought that comes from reaching out to God helps to relieve tension and give perspective, thus clearing the mind for the reception of beauty. Take the same walk in the woods when you are obsessed with a tantalizing problem, and you will see much less of the beauty of nature.

Looking again at our chosen definition of religious education, we see that we want to make available for our children *"the accumulated treasures of Christian life and thought in such a way that God in Christ may carry on His redemptive work in each human soul and in the common life of man."* Then let us respect every sign of growing religious life in our children, and, as we may learn from the wisdom of the Church, recognize the slow development from the cradle to the grave. We may ask ourselves whether the longing for God which is within every one of us from childhood, is helped or hindered by the religious education we offer.

Religious experience comes to almost all normal people, but few can be articulate about it. In referring to this in his wonderful essay, "Prayer and the Mystic Vision," Rufus Jones says, "It is, I maintain, the experience not only of rare and unusual personalities that a larger life impinges upon the margins of the inner realm, but most normal persons have at least moments when 'A bolt is shot back somewhere in the breast,' and they find themselves possessed of unsuspected energies, flooded with added life, as though a new compartment of being or a new dimension of space were opened, and they are inwardly convinced beyond all doubt that they have been in correspondence with a real though invisible world of Spirit and Life." Later he says, "The most positive contribution of the mystic to the world is *his own personal life,* heightened and dynamized by his inner experience." [3]

[3] From *Concerning Prayer,* p. 110, Macmillan. By permission.

Children and Religion

Not everyone can express, in later life, the experiences of childhood, but many can, thinking back, remember the stir of wonder and happiness that came through making the right decision in the face of difficulty, though not all see God in it. Others tell of similar experiences, sometimes during formal worship, often alone, when they have had their moments of "seeing God," and these times profoundly affect their idea of Him.

One child remembers wandering off from his friends when they were out blueberry-picking. He ran through a thicket of birch trees and young maples, where devil's paintbrushes and meadow rue and yellow loosestrife were growing, to the edge of a still lake. The water was so clear that the rocks shone up from below in clear colors. Busy insects went their way in the quiet, and a band of seagulls floated lazily over their fishing ground. The hills on the other side made an ark of shelter. He knew the place well, but never before had he caught the sense of pervading peace in all its fullness. Suddenly the familiar things seemed to have a radiance about them, and that glory was in some way bound up with the love of God in the universe. In that fleeting moment he saw into the inner side of life. He saw something of God, and resolved a conflict of unconscious ideas at war in his mind; he had a sense of ultimate good, that everything connected with us has another destination. Although a child, he knew the moment of insight could not go on. The other children called, and he ran back to resume the routine of his schoolboy existence, but he never forgot, and has said that the brief time of vision changed the whole course of his life; it became an integral part of the foundation of his faith in God as Creator, and later he came to know God acting as Redeemer, and Sanctifier, as Son and Holy Spirit.

Experience of God

Many feel that the high points are dangerous, and that the disillusion following the uplift is the time when faith is in greatest peril. But such revelations, coming through varying channels, can be united with the finding of God in the monotony of daily things, and the two stand together.

Let the aim of religious education be to lead the child to a vital experience of God, to rediscover the experience of transcendence. We adults can contribute very little, and yet we can contribute almost everything, in quality of life, and by leading the little child away from false conceptions of God. And from time to time, the child will reveal how far along the road it has travelled.

Some little time ago, when we were washing dishes, I put the question to a twelve-year-old girl that had just been put to me by an adult:

"What would you say to a person who says, 'I believe in God, but I can't believe that He'd care about *me*. Why should my little ways interest Him?' "

The child looked mildly surprised at the blindness of grown-ups, and said very simply, "But of course He's interested. It's just His greatness which makes Him understand: little things are great to Him."

We have hands that fashion and heads that know,
But our hearts we lost—how long ago!
In a place no chart nor ship can show
Under the sky's dome.

The world is wild as an old wives' tale
And strange the plain things are.
The earth is enough and the air is enough
For our wonder and our war;
But our rest is as far as the fire-drake swings

And our peace is put in impossible things
Where clashed and thundered unthinkable wings
Round an incredible star.

To an open house in the evening
Home shall men come,
To an older place than Eden
And a taller town than Rome.
To the end of the way of the wandering star,
To the things that cannot be and that are,
To the place where God was homeless
And all men are at home.[4]

[4] G. K. Chesterton, "The House of Christmas," *The Wild Knight and Other Poems*, Dutton.

INDEX

Index

A

Acland, Eleanor, 19, 189
activity, 49, 53, 59, 83, 120
adolescence, 7, 15, 18, 19, 22, 37, 46, 51
advertisements, 7, 25, 51, 153, 181
antipathy to religion, 34
art, 149, 157, 158, 184, 185, 219
atmosphere, 27, 34, 40, 91, 223
atomic bomb, 4, 5
attitude, 9, 10, 24, 27, 34, 48, 51, 60, 87, 92, 94, 150, 222, 224

B

Baldwin, A. Graham, 140, 149
beauty, 2, 10, 35, 40, 58, 228
bedtime, 32, 33, 63, 69, 143
belief, 197
Bible, The, 117ff, 126, 190
    English Bible, 121, 123, 124
    King James Version, 89, 116, 124
    Revised Standard Version, 130
    Vulgate, The, 121
    Wycliffe Bible, 122
Bible and The Common Reader, The, 126n, 128
"Bobby Sox Religion," 55
body, the, 76, 80
books, 155ff, 188ff, 191
    children's, 188
    picture, 156
    poetry, 170ff
    religious, 189, 190
Bremner, Vivyen, 30, 192
Burdekin, Harold, 65, 191

C

camp, 35, 150, 153, 228
Case, Adelaide T., 21, 146, 174
change, 5, 72, 77, 92
Chase, Mary Ellen, 125, 128
choice, 51, 52
Christian Family, 34
Christianity, 7, 8, 50, 150, 203, 214, 215, 226
Christmas, 39, 40, 41, 105, 161, 209, 210
church, 34, 81
civilization, 1, 4, 6, 10, 71, 116, 125, 149, 186, 217, 226
college, 7, 20
comics, 25, 152ff
community, 21, 53, 72, 83
compromise, 152
conferences, 47, 48, 55, 112
conversion, 101
cooperation, 104, 105, 206
Coverdale, 123
creation, 78, 150
criticism, 22, 25, 153, 208
    Higher Criticism, 37, 190, 225
    historical, 117, 118
curiosity, 212, 213
curriculum, 135, 136

D

death, 8, 42, 75ff, 80, 81, 85, 218
destiny, 89, 150
disbelief, 197ff
disillusionment, 46

Index

Index

hymns, 161, 165
hypocrisy, 70

I

imagination, 131, 133, 156, 174
immortality, 76, 77
individual, 13, 51, 73, 91, 228
influence, 10, 50, 60, 89, 221
intellectual, 3, 4, 215
intercession, prayers of, 67, 69

J

Jacks, L. P., 196, 214
Jewish, 38, 103, 203
Jones, Rufus, 217, 229
Junior, 16, 17, 36, 37, 38
Jung, C. G., 2, 13, 14
juvenile delinquency, 6, 151

K

Kingdom of God, 49
knowledge, 4, 11, 37, 45, 227

L

laws, 2, 13, 36, 116, 117, 204, 218
legend, 16, 37, 43
life, 2, 3, 10, 13, 14, 25, 40, 77, 219
Livingstone, Sir Richard, 1, 3, 168
love of God, 40, 72, 223

M

magazines, 80, 118, 152ff, 202
materialism, 8, 49, 88, 127, 148, 149, 188
maturity, 13, 23, 68, 69, 73, 226
memorizing, 143

miracles, 199, 211, 212
movies, 7, 25, 51, 80, 118, 150, 153, 169, 181, 188
music, 40, 60, 63, 166
    appreciation, 161, 185
    religious, 161, 165
mysticism, 60, 61, 149, 217, 229
myths, 16, 37, 206

N

nature, 35, 229
need, 13, 21, 36, 49, 61, 143, 184

P

peach, 9, 24, 218
personality, 10, 13, 21, 23, 27, 51, 58, 60, 78, 218, 223
Petersham, Maud and Miska, 39, 193
petition, 67, 68, 69
pictures, 25, 156
poetry, 37, 38, 40, 71, 166ff, 169, 170ff, 171, 172
power, 49, 56, 149, 150, 218
Pratt, Prof. J. B., 46, 60, 224
prayer, 58, 62, 63, 66, 67, 68, 69, 72, 73, 220
    Prayer Book, 107
press, 7, 25, 51, 169
pretense, 60
propaganda, 50, 51, 52
Psalms, 172
psychology, 2, 4, 7, 9, 12, 60, 218
punishment, 70

Q

Quakers, The, 72
question, 29, 42, 77, 199, 209, 212
quiet time, 32
quietude, 33

Index